BY DAVID E. SMITH

John Bunyan in America

John Bunyan in America

THE PILGRIM'S PROGRESS

Second Part, Boston, 1744

Woodcut from English prototypes. Such allegorical representation of Christian's journey was common in both English and American editions.

by David E. Smith

John Bunyan in America

Bloomington
INDIANA UNIVERSITY PRESS
London

Indiana University Humanities Series Number 61
Indiana University, Bloomington, Indiana

EDITOR: Edward D. Seeber
ASSISTANT EDITOR: David H. Dickason
ASSISTANT EDITOR: Hubert C. Heffner

The Indiana University Humanities Series was founded in 1939 for the publication of occasional papers and monographs by members of the faculty.

Library of Congress Catalog Card No. 65-65119

TO

Priscilla

PREFACE

READERS of the present study will be struck by the absence of discussion of many major literary figures including Franklin, Emerson, Thoreau, Melville, Whitman, and others. Franklin's youthful interest in Bunyan, and the "Pilgrim's-Progress" pattern of his autobiography have been discussed recently by Charles Sanford in *The Quest for Paradise.* As for the others, I have followed a general policy of limitation which seemed necessary in a study of this nature: unless the reflection of Bunyan in their mature work seemed pervasive and measurably direct, I felt obliged to ignore them. The dangerous assumption in a study of this kind (and one which I hope I am not guilty of in my treatment of Hawthorne, the Alcotts, Cummings, and others) is that any use of the pilgrimage theme, or any frequent use of allegory, suggests *a priori* a reflection of Bunyan. Melville's *Pierre* may be, as a great Melville scholar once suggested to me, a *Pilgrim's Progress* in reverse, Walden Pond may be the Celestial City: but I must insist that mine is a conservative study of Bunyan's influence—it is not a book about the theme of pilgrimage in America, except indirectly, although such a book might well be written.

I am indebted to the Graduate School of Indiana University for a grant which enabled me to bring this study to its present form. The Graduate School of the University of Minnesota enabled me, through a grant-in-aid, to examine Bunyaniana in a number of American libraries. In particular, the staffs of the Library of the American Antiquarian Society and the New York Public Library were generous of their time and aid.

Mr. Clifford K. Shipton, Director of the American Antiquarian Society, allowed me the honor of examining the most complete collection of early American editions of the works of Bunyan that exists. Mr. Lewis M. Stark, Chief of the Rare Book Division, The New York Public Library, and his assistant Mrs. Maud Cole, aided me immeasurably.

I should also like to acknowledge the permission given me by the editors of *Twentieth Century Literature* (July, 1965) to reproduce in this monograph portions of Chapter V that first appeared in that publication.

Any number of antiquarian book dealers dealt kindly with me, and I owe a special debt of gratitude to Mr. Francis J. O'Brien, of Portland, Maine, whose early and continued interest in my researches has been of great aid to me.

I wish to thank Professor Jacob Levenson of the University of Minnesota for his patient efforts as first director of this study in its early forms, and Professor Bernard Bowron for his willingness to continue its direction. Professor Leo Marx was a patient and helpful reader.

To Professor Samuel Holt Monk I would say that "what my jury be, I know not; but 'tis good for a criminal to plead before a favorable judge. If I had said partial, would your Lordship have forgiven me? Or will you give me leave to acquaint the world that I have many times been oblig'd to your bounty. . . . ?"

My gratitude to my wife, Priscilla Riley Smith, cannot be properly expressed. Without her, this study would never have been begun, worried over, or completed.

CONTENTS

ILLUSTRATIONS

FACING PAGE 105

The Pilgrim's Progress, Philadelphia, M'Culloch, 1793. Reproduced by permission of the Princeton University Library from the Sinclair Hamilton Collection, No. 146.

I

My Pilgrim's Book has travell'd sea and land,
Yet could I never come to understand
That it was slighted, or turn'd out of door
By any Kingdom, were they rich or poor.
  In France and Flanders, where men kill each other,
My Pilgrim is esteem'd a Friend, a Brother.
  In Holland, too, 'tis said, as I am told,
My Pilgrim is with some worth more than Gold.
  Highlanders and Wild Irish can agree
My Pilgrim should familiar with them be.
  'Tis in New England under such advance,
Receives there so much loving countenance,
As to be trimm'd, new cloth'd, and deck't with Gems,
That it may shew its features and its limbs,
Yet more, so comely doth my Pilgrim walk
That of him thousands daily sing and talk.

———JOHN BUNYAN, in "The Author's Way of Sending Forth His Second Part of the 'Pilgrim.' "

To blend instruction with delight,
Mankind the easier to excite,
To love the things that are divine;
Was B U N Y A N ' S *great and good design.*

THE PILGRIM'S PROGRESS
Philadelphia, M'Culloch, 1793

This may represent the earliest known work of the American woodcut artist Alexander Anderson. See David Smith, "Illustrations of American Editions of *The Pilgrim's Progress* to 1870," *Princeton University Library Chronicle* (Autumn, 1964).

the one hand with the eastern seaboard and its developing commerce, and on the other hand with the still considerable stretches of back-country wilderness, Morgan chose his setting "in that part of Basaruah [allegorically "flesh-spirit"] which lies toward the North of America" (p. 33). It is a poor barren country, even at best, says the narrator—a messenger of the Lord sent as a kind of observer. The basic metaphor of Morgan's tale is that of a vast tract of wilderness through which some few paths lead, and on the borders of which flows a broad body of water forming an impassable barrier. The task of the disinherited inhabitants of this virtually impenetrable wilderness consists mainly of weeding out its poisonous plants and subduing its wild beasts. The King of the country had marked out a path through the wilderness to the "Pleasant Country" (p. 67), "but the people were grown so perverse with eating the wild fruits" (p. 68) that they would go off the narrow path in search of them. Seventeenth- and eighteenth-century Englishmen regarded gardens by and large as places of refuge and symbols of order. Gardens, as much as architecture or other artifacts, may be regarded as reflections of men's minds, especially of their tastes. For Englishmen in the age of Dryden—including Puritans—the diametrical opposite of a garden would be a wilderness. Thus, for Puritans, the term wilderness invariably signifies chaos. What one does *with* a wilderness when one is confronted with it and cannot escape it is amply illustrated in the case of the early generations of Puritan settlers, who "fenced it out." Wilderness implied wildness, beasts, poison, savages. If one must venture into the wilderness it should be to change it into a garden: that is, to weed out and destroy its "poisonous fruits," and to destroy or domesticate its savage beasts.[8]

Morgan's allegory is a study of the various ways in

which the inhabitants of Basaruah made their way toward the Celestial City, despite the impediments and obstacles to their progress. It relies as much upon Bunyan's *Holy War* as upon *The Pilgrim's Progress,*[9] but its special interest for us in this discussion lies in its incorporation of ideas which anticipate much later "uses" of Bunyan in America. First, it relies on (and recommends for further amplification) Bunyan's own works, employing his familiar allegorical techniques; second, it applies these techniques to the basic tenets of Calvinistic doctrine such as predestination, election, and perseverance of the saints; third, it adapts these allegorical devices to a new setting, namely, the American wilderness, thereby introducing a totally new factor into the Bunyan "formula"; fourth, it introduces the conception of the millennium as a central doctrine. Although the unrepentant would most certainly perish in a "Sulpherous Lake of Fire and Brimstone" on the Day of Judgment, Morgan claimed salvation for large numbers through the intervention of a predicted millennium: "Since I was in the Country, and before the Great General Court, there was a period of time called *Ta Chilia Ete* [The Thousand Years], wherein the Prince was Resolved to shew to all the world his Power and Conquest over the Rebellious Ruhoths [spirits] who managed continual War against him in Basaruah" (p. 155). During the period of *Ta Chilia Ete,* the elect were able to go to every corner of the wilderness, capture all rebels, kill all the wild beasts, and cut up all the wild fruits. More people crossed the River of Regeneration during this period than "all that went to the *Sulpherous Pit* before that time . . ." (p. 157). With this prophetic assertion, Morgan concludes *The Kingdom of Basaruah,* warning his contemporaries to "consider these things, if you love your lives." Morgan's is the first application by an American writer of the doctrines, lessons, and allegorical technique of Bunyan to the colonial experience. When Bunyan had spoken of the "wilderness of this world" in the famous opening to his allegory, he could not possibly have conceived of the impact which an actual physical wilderness would have upon the Puritan imagination.[10] Morgan's *Kingdom of Basaruah* is the first of a number of American books which attempt to encompass the wilderness imaginatively, and yet at the same time sustain the weight of Calvinistic doctrinal meaning through the technique of allegory.

Such a use of Bunyan's works to fortify millennial ideas is not surprising. Bunyan himself, as I have suggested, betrayed strong millenarian tendencies throughout his life, and, as one recent critic has astutely observed, *The Pilgrim's Progress* itself reflects "the social ideals of a Christian utopia, with all the revolutionary implications of establishing Christ's kingdom on earth, later amplified in [the] *Holy War*."[11]

Morgan's "Ta Chilia Ete" is one of a number of hopeful American millennial utopias contrived during this period. Morgan was in correspondence with Cotton Mather, and may well have been familiar with Mather's *magnum opus* on the subject, in which the City of God would appear in New England following the imminent ruin of Antichrist.[12]

Allegory lends itself easily to schemes involving the "resurrection of Lost Paradises,"[13] and Morgan's allegory shares both the seriousness and the awkwardness of the pastoral form as it incongruously reshapes the baffling American wilderness into a utopian garden. *The Kingdom of Basaruah* anticipates later and somewhat more sophisticated treatments of the same theme, for numerous nineteenth-century American allegories repeatedly placed Bunyan's Christian in an American wilderness and made him tramp through it in search of the Celestial City. If the genre received its consummate treatment by Hawthorne, his forebear was Joseph Morgan.

HIGHWAYS AND BYWAYS

The force of the primitive American environment was at once the baffling and the shaping element in Morgan's kingdom, and it was with such a force that later allegorists were to wrestle as they strove to adapt the ever-popular *Pilgrim's Progress* to an American setting. Even in Bunyan's day the idea of byways and their inevitable pitfalls was solidly invested with its own meaning. In medieval England, Jerusalem, or a Jerusalem-substitute, waited inevitably at the end of a pilgrimage-way, but, as Muriel Bowden[14] and others have pointed out, and as we observe for ourselves so vividly in Chaucer, the congruous aspect of pleasure-seeking *on the way*—as a perfectly fit part of pilgrimaging—eventually became for many pilgrims the object of pilgrimage "in Aprille." Byways, therefore, often involved sophisticated, civilized, and satisfying forms of temptation. Conversely, when the pilgrimage was transferred to the American continent, it was confronted by an environment radically dissimilar to that of the conventional English pilgrimages. Jerusalem no longer waited at the end of the difficult way: if it were to appear, it must be created, constructed, shaped. The Heavenly City emerged, as it were, to the degree that a satanic wilderness was torn away and subdued. Since the "path" customarily and naturally moved through the virgin land in a western direction, it followed that the New Jerusalem would be at the frontier or "vaguely realizing westward." Consequently, the path itself through the wilderness, which in medieval England and elsewhere had become increasingly attractive *because* of its byways, was stripped bare of pleasures for the American pilgrim-wanderer. The harsh realities of severe climate, hostile Indians, and a literally trackless wilderness were a direct, not a veiled, revelation of Satan. Frederick Jackson Turner suggested that the area of free land to the west was a powerful force shaping American character. However, a peculiar American attitude toward the frontier, and the pilgrimage through it, shaped the frontier in the imagination of those who experienced it either literally or figuratively, and perhaps gave impetus to the shaping of the frontier into a garden, a process which, first of all, involved ridding the New Eden of Satan.

Nathaniel Hawthorne, as we shall see, turned repeatedly in his fiction to the image of pathways through a wilderness. The kind of pilgrims who interested Hawthorne, and the nature of his pilgrimage, received definition *via* the wilderness itself into which Hawthorne placed his characters. Hawthorne's imaginary wilderness—his bewildering and trackless forest—is indigenously American, not European. Some didactic and less capable writers than Hawthorne, whose works I shall examine in the next chapter, were nevertheless confronted by the same problem when they placed a Bunyan-like Christian in a contemporary American setting.

It is worth a speculative guess that in later times, when the wilderness had been all but "subdued" in the Turnerian sense, when cities had sprung up, and roads been built, the pilgrimage did not vanish but instead assumed a new character, as did the pilgrim himself. The image of the road has for so long lent itself conventionally to the concept of quest and pilgrimage—with some version of the Holy City at its end—that it can rarely be dissociated from that idea. In modern literature, the roadway becomes a thing in itself, usually leading nowhere in particular, and a new figure—the hobo-clown[15]—supplants the traditional burdened pilgrim. Whitman's open-throated singer, weary of cities, on the open road leading westward, anticipates a series of dispossessed wanderers. The outcast, however, becomes the truly holy pilgrim in exile and appears as such in *In Our Time*, *The Grapes of Wrath*, *U.S.A.*, not to mention such figures in the works of Anderson, Faulkner, Warren, Hart Crane, and others. The dispossessed hobo-clown, wandering down an endless stretch of pavement past the edges of cities, becomes a central figure in modern literature. When the American wilderness had vanished, the conventional figure of Bunyan's Christian in America vanished also. There was no sanction or authority for him, although, ironically, Vanity Fair remained unchanged. In the nineteenth century, however, conditions of belief and convention allowed for a curious collection of "Christians" making their way through an alien American society, commenting, as they traveled, upon its customs from a traditionally Calvinistic bias. Theological modernism, reform, transcendental optimism—even science and "progress"—were mercilessly and repeatedly attacked in the American "Pilgrim's Progresses." An apocalyptic temperament, combined with a stubborn faith in an imminent millennium, characterizes this American Bunyan literature. When, by the third quarter of the century, it was obvious that no cataclysmic event,[16] such as the hoped-for millennium, would occur, the American pilgrim was left to wander unprepared and dispossessed in a world he hardly understood. "The path," as Henry Adams was to discover, "led nowhere."[17] Every Christian, of course, in Bunyan's sense, must exile himself from his familiar world, and choose to forsake even wife and family to quit the City of Destruction and follow the narrow way to the Celestial City. But whereas in Bunyan's allegory the way is clearly marked, and the byways, however tempting, are properly understood to be byways, the individual wanderer, by the second half of the nineteenth century in America, was stranded on a roadway—paved (or railed) though it may have been—which led nowhere. "Faith held out, but the paths grew dim. . . . The weary pilgrim [was led] into such mountains of ignorance that he could no longer see any path whatever, and could not even understand a signpost."[18]

APOCALYPSE AND REFORM

John Oman, in *The Natural and the Supernatural*, has distinguished between the mystical and the apocalyptic in religion by saying that: "In the former case the eternal is sought as the unchanging by escape from the evanescent; in the latter it is looked for in the evanescent as a revelation of the increasing purpose in its changes."[19] The mystical, that is, "seeks the eternal behind the illusion of the evanescent," whereas the apocalyptic "looks for a revealing in the evanescent." Bunyan himself was an apocalyptic dreamer, but his prison experiences seem to have altered his earlier apocalypticism to the degree that *The Pilgrim's Progress* represents a balance between the mystical and the apocalyptic. Nineteenth-century American Calvinists and others interested in Bunyan sought the apocalyptic rather than the mystical, built utopias out of a desire to speed the advent of the millennium, and nationalized and particularized their millennial hopes. This was at once a constructive and a destructive act. The destruction of the present wicked generation would be apocalyptic; the construction of the New Jerusalem on American soil would be an example of revelation in the evanescent.

Hawthorne's personal experience with reformers, culminating in his distress at Brook Farm, resulted in an artistic attempt to destroy the entire world of reform. Ultimately, however, he perceived that the bleak, post-Doomsday world inhabited by a "new" but lonely Adam and Eve would be little better than a Vanity Fair heavily populated by sinners. A near-endorsement, in *The House of the Seven Gables,* of Holgrave's somewhat overweening optimism,[20] is supplanted a year later in the next novel by Coverdale's wavering position at Blithedale, nicely figured by his pine-tree hideaway; but Hawthorne is not the narrator in *The Blithedale Romance,* and in Coverdale, he created what had by then become in his work a characteristic figure: the disingenuous pilgrim trapped in an ambiguous world midway between the forsaken City of Destruction and the sought-after Celestial City. Bunyan's Ignorance stands at the center of Hawthorne's art.

I suggest, then, that American interest in Bunyan was reflected in rather special and often curious ways. The American wilderness became a symbol for dark, Satanic evil. The process of cultivating it into a garden required, from a Puritan standpoint, clearing, weeding, and fencing in. A Bunyan-like pilgrim, placed incongruously in this new wilderness world, in contradistinction to Bunyan's "wilderness of this world," would wander in a maze, as do, for example, Reuben Bourne in "Roger Malvin's Burial," Arthur Dimmesdale, Miles Coverdale, and Clifford Pyncheon. A tendency to regard modern reform movements with conservative suspicion is reflected in numerous American "Pilgrim's Progresses," but the countertendency to reconstruct Jerusalem in a pastoral setting, usually upon the ashes left by a cleansing, apocalyptic fire, is also fundamental in most American Bunyan literature.

THE CIVIL WAR AND AFTER

This brings me to a final consideration in my introductory remarks: the slavery question and the Civil War itself. The events of the forties and fifties stimulated a rather curious and distorted "use" of Bunyan by Abolitionist writers. As a conflict appeared more and more inevitable (to the Abolitionists, at any rate), it came to be regarded as a kind of Holy War, and ultimately to be associated, in some circles, with the imagery of Gog and Magog, the binding of Satan, and other lurid symbolism from the Apocalypse. It was probably inevitable, therefore, that Calvinistic liberators of the more colorful sort would turn to Bunyan's *Holy War* and *Pilgrim's Progress* as readily available sources of imagery for their purposes. The application of these works to such a specific issue as slavery had its ludicrous aspects, to be sure, but those nearest the issues could hardly have understood them at the time. As early as 1843, and coincidental with the publication of Hawthorne's "Celestial Railroad," appeared a full-length Abolitionist work entitled *Pilgrim's Progress in the Last Days* in which the entire Holy War is fought in gruesome detail, the antagonists being Christian Abolition and the Giant Slavery. One of the most vituperative of the Abolitionists, the Reverend George B. Cheever of the Church of the Pilgrims in New York City, a lifelong Bunyan-worshipper, impressed his hero into service in the fight against slavery. How Bunyan was enlisted in the cause of Abolitionism is discussed in detail below. It remains for me to call attention to a reaction against him which seems to have taken place in America after the war.

Until the Civil War, *The Pilgrim's Progress* continued a lively best-seller, reaching the height of its popularity in the 1840's. After the war there was a marked decline in the number of annual editions. Furthermore, although Bunyan was not soon forgotten in this country, abruptly at this period he seems to have become, for the first time, fit subject for parody and travesty. It is as if the war marked a period before which Bunyan was always taken seriously, and after which he was rarely taken seriously. Evidence for this shift in attitude toward Bunyan is provided in my discussion of *Little Women* in Chapter Four. Needless to say, the year 1870 did not bring American interest in Bunyan, or the reflection of his influence, to a close. *The Pilgrim's Progress* will probably always find readers in America; however, a massive influence upon a society is a different thing from a minor influence upon sects or individuals, and the period around 1870 marks a shift in the latter direction.

II

19TH-CENTURY AMERICAN ADAPTATIONS OF *THE PILGRIM'S PROGRESS* TO 1855

The attempts which have been made to improve and to imitate *The Pilgrim's Progress* are not to be numbered. It has been done into verse; it has been done into modern English. *The Pilgrimage of Tender Conscience,* the *Pilgrimage of Good Intent,* the *Pilgrimage of Seek Truth,* the *Pilgrimage of Theophilus,* the *Infant Pilgrim,* the *Hindoo Pilgrim,* are among the many feeble copies of the great original. But the peculiar glory of Bunyan is that those who most hated his doctrines have tried to borrow the help of his genius. A Roman Catholic version of his parable may be seen with the head of the virgin in the title-page.

———THOMAS BABINGTON MACAULAY

Behold here now the Slothful are a Sign,
Hung up, 'cause Holy Ways they did decline:
See here too how the Child doth play the Man,
And Weak grows Strong, when Great-Heart leads the Van.

THE PILGRIM'S PROGRESS

Great-Heart conducting Christiana and her family (This is a possible visual source for Hawthorne's Hollingsworth in *The Blithedale Romance.*)

Chapter Two

MACAULAY'S dictum bears repeating, and, as might be expected, American (as well as English) "improvements" of *The Pilgrim's Progress* are rife. But if the imitations have occasionally degenerated to the level of the absurd as in *Bob's Hike to the Holy City*, or *Two Pilgrims' Progress to Fair Florence* (on a bicycle), they have also reached the level of superb satire in "The Celestial Railroad." Hawthorne's imaginative adaptation of *The Pilgrim's Progress* to a contemporary American setting is in our day the only familiar one. In his day, however, "The Celestial Railroad" was hardly an innovation, and what saved it from the oblivion of similar works were Hawthorne's genius and renown. Edwin Honig has recently suggested that allegory in our day suffers from a pervasive feeling against it: "the feeling is that allegory lends itself to polemical purposes and therefore turns inevitably into an exercise of subliterary fancies."[1] In an earlier day, allegory was not so universally mistrusted, and if its purpose was often polemical, it yet spoke with some authority to a wider audience which was conditioned to appreciate its subtleties. Hawthorne's continual reliance (not merely in "The Celestial Railroad") upon allegorical methods was a result, at least in part, of his appreciation of an audience of readers who, like himself, had been nurtured upon Bunyan. This audience was also assumed by the authors of other American improvisations upon *The Pilgrim's Progress.* What most of these works have in common is the enemy; liberalism. What some of them, unfortunately, are not blessed with, is the sustaining force of genius in their rendering. A common suspicion of progress and reform pervades all of the works, including Hawthorne's. The following survey is intended as preparatory to an analysis of Hawthorne's "The Celestial Railroad," but it also demonstrates the immense popularity of *The Pilgrim's Progress* and anything remotely connected with it during the first half of the nineteenth century in America, while it suggests that forces of theological conservatism found in Bunyan's work a valuable weapon in their desperate Holy War.

The Pilgrim's Progress in the Nineteenth Century

William R. Weeks' *The Pilgrim's Progress in the Nineteenth Century* grew out of its author's conviction that every conceivable effort must be made to stem the tide of liberal doctrine which was, in his opinion, endangering the older Calvinistic faith in America. The final edition of the work, published in 1849, "elucidate[s]," in the opinion of one reviewer, "the history and course of religious opinion and practice in this country during the past thirty years."[2] A Newark editor advised that "readers who remember anything of the fanatical and virulent excitements which prevailed in the various parts of the State of New York a few years ago . . . will be especially struck [by Weeks' arguments]. . . ."[3] The history of the book's publication reflects Weeks' life-long struggle with forces he conceived to be destructive of orthodox Presbyterian doctrine. Originally issued under the pseudonym "Bunyanus" in the *Utica Christian Repository* during the years 1824–

26, reprinted in the *Christian Magazine*, 1825–1827, the work was issued in two small volumes in 1826 in New York. In 1849, a year after Weeks' death, an enlarged version appeared in New York and Boston under his name, acknowledging that he was the author of the earlier versions also.

Within its dogmatic and digressive pages, the book attacks mesmerism, witchcraft, fairs, light reading, comic pictures, intemperance, slavery, theaters, and Sabbath-breaking. The means of introducing these multitudinous evils is the journey of Thoughtful—a nineteenth-century counterpart of Bunyan's Christian—and his faithful companion Ardent. In their extensive travels throughout North America, these two pilgrims (evidently representing Weeks' conception of utterly orthodox Presbyterianism) are exposed to such dangers as those listed above, as well as to the principal examples of heterodoxy and heresy understood by Weeks to exist in America during the first half of the nineteenth century. An illustration is the Giant Presumption, who had done "unspeakably more mischief than was ever done by Giant Despair":

> Though a giant in strength, he prevails more by his subtilty. He calls himself, and is called by his followers *Great Faith.* You will meet with his emissaries under many names and disguises. Perfectionists, Unionists, Campbellites, Millerites, Annihilators, Universalists, Mormons, Transcendentalists, Swedenborgians, Fourierites, Anti-punishment men, & c., all engage harmoniously in his service. Having filled the region formerly occupied by Giant Despair, it is thought he is aiming to get possession of the Delectable Mountains. [p. 484]

Weeks reserved his most virulent attacks for heresy within the fold. *The Pilgrim's Progress in the Nineteenth Century* is a study in allegorical form of the conflicts which arose within the Presbyterian hierarchy in the late 1820's. These conflicts had been dramatized by the church's attack on a Reverend Barnes of Morristown as an Arminian in 1829; a Reverend Duffield of Carlisle in 1832, for his views on regeneration; and had reached their peak with the all-out attack on Dr. Lyman Beecher, who was arraigned in 1835 on the charge of doctrinal error. Beecher was accused of teaching "Pelagian and Arminian doctrine in respect to Free Agency, Original Sin, Total Depravity, Regeneration, and Christian Character, etc.";[4] and although he was vindicated, his "trial" reflects the intensity of the conflict which had arisen between the newer Home Missionary Society (of the Presbyterian Church) and the Presbyterian Assembly's own "Board on the Western field." The conflict had developed in the 1820's, when professors at the recently formed and highly orthodox Andover Theological Seminary challenged the teaching at the Theological Seminary in New Haven. Exhibiting growing alarm at the "dangerous errors"[5] generating out of New Haven and spreading to the West, and conceiving that the seminary at New Haven was the "fountain-head of heresy," the Drs. Woods, Griffin, and Tyler openly expressed their growing apprehensions. Mr. Nettleton, also of Andover, in a letter to Dr. Plumer, confessed that he was deeply distressed at the "loose speculations which [have] come from the New Haven school and from Mr. Finney and others of that stamp" (p. 458). Charles Grandison Finney was, of course, the type of the free-swinging "western" evangelist. The Andover men, disregarding the "results" of his sweeping revivals, disapproved highly of his methods.

Weeks is best understood within this context. He was born in Brooklyn, Connecticut, in 1783. Upon graduation from Princeton in 1809, he studied at Andover Theological Seminary, after which he was pastor of Presbyterian churches in New York State from 1812 to 1832, when he moved to New Jersey. Thus he was in a strategic position to observe the developing conflict between the orthodox and the "heretical" factions in the church. This conflict is expressed in his book through the two preachers, Mr. Meek and Mr. Bold. Mr. Meek, whose church is on Pilgrim Street, preached a "plain, scriptural discourse on the lost and ruined state of man by nature. Having carefully explained his doctrine, and guarded it against misapprehension, he proceeded to supplement it by arguments drawn directly from the King's book" (p. 208). In Mr. Meek's sermons there were no "loud and boisterous tones, no theatrical gesticulations, no rhetorical flourishes" (p. 208). In contrast, Mr. Bold, whose church is on Westerly Street, employed the "machinery of the theatre" (p. 234) to stimulate his congregation. He is "very familiar" in his pastoral prayer, "as if the suppliant had forgotten his station, and was talking with an equal" (p. 234). Whereas Mr. Bold is considered to be an Arminian (p. 271) and praised for his Arminian views by his followers, Mr. Meek continually quotes The Presbyterian General Assembly, President Dwight of Yale, and Jonathan Edwards to bolster his arguments. Mr. Meek is also contrasted with the famous evangelist Whitefield: "[Mr. Meek was not as] eloquent as Whitefield, [and] as a natural consequence, the revivals which occur[red] under his preaching [were] more pure, attended with less fanaticism, and a smaller proportion of contemporary converts" (p. 217). Mr. Meek and Mr. Bold are by no means the only prominent figures in the battle. Mr. Bold's advocates feel that "Calvinism has seen its best days, no doubt" (p. 271). The "modern" preacher, if he is not a western evangelist who inspires his listeners to exclaim "I call that *preaching*, gentlemen, don't you?" is a slick operator like the New York preachers

Dr. Smoothman, Dr. Soothing, Mr. Slight-heal, and Mr. Save-all. Dr. Smoothman might best be described as an early Norman Vincent Peale. His advice to the spiritually distressed person is: "Banish all . . . thoughts [which occasion] distress, and avoid everything which is likely to suggest them. Divert your mind, don't dwell on gloomy subjects. . . . Resort to some harmless amusement. . . . Read some diverting book, such as a novel or a play" (p. 18). Weeks' gallery of heretical and heterodoxical believers is elaborate, curious, and grotesque. So bent was he upon his mission of saving the world by his own narrow dogmatism, he lacked what might have been a saving humility. For example, although he acknowledged that Bunyan's *Pilgrim's Progress* contributed more than any other work "to give form to [his] mind and direction to [his] thoughts," he added that his own later theological study showed him "some mistakes into which Bunyan had fallen," and he set out before he was thirty to write a *Pilgrim's Progress* "in which those mistakes should be avoided" (p. iii). The result is often an overdose of Presbyterian doctrine at the expense of narrative interest. Nevertheless, Weeks' satirical wit occasionally sparkles, as in his description of a typical lady of fashion of the day, who presides as hostess of a "modern" House Beautiful: "We are extremely anxious to cultivate our pious feelings. We carefully avoid all addresses to the understanding, as likely to cool the ardor of our devotion. We do not wish to *think*,—we wish to *feel*" (p. 58). In Feel-well, another character, Weeks successfully portrays the supersentimental worshipper: "I want a religion that I can feel. Glory to the King! Glory to the Prince who died for me! Glory! Glory!" And in Liberal, who deems himself the lineal descendant of Gaius (who had entertained Christiana and her children), "the host of the church," Weeks created a successful portrait of a champion of religious progress at any cost: "We agree to differ. . . . The pilgrim world are now engaging in great enterprises for advancing the kingdom of the Lord, and as many hands must be called to the work, we feel it of great importance to cultivate a spirit of harmony and good feeling among all denominations . . ." (p. 156).

Weeks was one of a number of ministers troubled by the direction of thought represented in Deism, Unitarianism, and other "free-thinking" theologies. From his first publications, such as "Withholding a suitable support from the ministers of religion is robbing God . . . ," and "A Catechism of Scripture Doctrine," Weeks demonstrated his unshakable faith in the hard Calvinistic line taught him at Andover, and like a fellow-scholar at that institution, Hawthorne's classmate at Bowdoin, George Barrell Cheever, he found in *The Pilgrim's Progress* an ideal weapon with which to attack those writings and institutions in his own time that he regarded as dangerously heretical.

Pilgrim's Progress in the Last Days

The unidentified author of the little-known *Pilgrim's Progress in the Last Days*[6] ingeniously combined almost all of the elements which would be present, in one form or another, in subsequent American "Pilgrim's Progresses." Furthermore, he succeeded, as only Hawthorne was otherwise to succeed,[7] in dramatizing these elements sufficiently to save his allegory from becoming merely a succession of pious sermons. Thus, *Pilgrim's Progress in the Last Days* should be regarded as a prototype.[8] Not only does it retrace Christian's steps through the allegorical country of Bunyan's original, making each place applicable to America in the nineteenth century, but it encompasses, in its broad sweep, attacks upon almost every institution which would be subsequently attacked in similar but less effective works.

The book is noteworthy for many reasons besides the universality of its attack. In the first place, as its title would indicate, it is specifically millennial in theme. It describes in detail the fiery destruction of the world (specifically America) and clearly anticipates the thousand-year rule of Christ on the new earth purged by fire. In the second place, it devotes more space to an extended and ingenious analysis of and attack on Negro slavery than does any other work of this nature, ascribes political and economic reasons for the existence of slavery,[9] and predicts the "irrepressible conflict," making the war between North and South part of a larger battle which anticipates the coming of the Last Days. The work, moreover, scrutinizes and derogates certain aspects of conservatism, while most of the other works of this type limit their attacks to theological liberalism alone. In addition, it successfully allegorizes certain conventional objects of attack less successfully treated in the other works, including transcendentalism, classical humanism, and progress as reflected in a contemporary faith in modern science and invention.[10] Finally, *Pilgrim's Progress in the Last Days* succeeds because in general its allegory is effectively sustained; the author is obviously more a craftsman than a moralizer, and he rarely allows his message to interfere with the narrative to such a degree that the reader entirely loses interest.

Seen in perspective, however, *Pilgrim's Progress in the Last Days* is a work which demonstrates to what degree Bunyan's allegory could be distorted in the interests of special pleading. The idea—no matter how ingenious—of proslavery spies taking pot-shots at abolitionists out of the windows of a much-decayed House Beautiful; or even more spectacular, of Christian accompanied on his journey by a fugitive slave called White-heart (and spurned consequently by such fellow-travelers as Prejudice and Discontent), demonstrates vividly what had become of Bunyan in America before the Civil War. Because of its immense general popularity, *The Pilgrim's Progress* was used as a weapon, and because of the very special nature of the "enemy," the wielders of this weapon apparently cared little about anything except its effectiveness in battle. However, this is all the more reason why *Pilgrim's Progress in the Last Days* is a prototype: every American adaptation of *The Pilgrim's Progress* which I have examined shares the same intention, employs similar themes, and utilizes similar devices.[11]

Of the many objects of attack in *Pilgrim's Progress in the Last Days,* perhaps slavery can best be singled out for discussion. There is little indication in the first fifty pages of the book that it will suddenly explode into a violent abolitionist tract, unless one pauses over the description of Christian himself as being of "dark hue" (p. 23). The antislavery theme is not introduced until some twenty pages later, and then it comes on us abruptly. In the preceding narrative, Christian has avoided the bridge over the Slough of Despond, encountered a character named Liberal who wishes to introduce him to his friend, Dr. Rational, stopped at the Interpreter's House (where he is shown the figure of Napoleon, among other instructive sights, standing on a pyramid of human skulls), climbed Hill Difficulty (which is "steeper than ever" [p. 30]), and arrived at a deteriorated Palace Beautiful—the entrance to which is now a broad avenue unguarded by lions! While Christian dines with some of the new residents of the House—including Mr. Church-patronage, "a man of great stature and increasing bulk" (p. 41), Mr. Conformity, and Mr. Expediency—an "ethiopian" (who is in fact a fugitive slave) dashes into the House pleading for refuge. An argument ensues between Mr. Expediency, who washes his hands of the whole business because "we shall only get ourselves into trouble" (p. 53), and a man of "bold and resolute countenance" named Christian Abolition, who not only stands up for the fugitive slave, but suggests to the assembled company that it is time to break up the castle of the monster who for so many ages has made Negroes into slaves: the Giant Slavery. Conformity denounces Christian Abolition, claiming that "things are much exaggerated" (p. 54) as to the Giant's reputation. Mr. Expediency gets to the heart of the matter when he says that he knows many of the sons of the Giant who are nice people, arguing that by alienating the sons of the Giant, "we shall lose all the wealth they bring us" (p. 55). However, the debate is won by the forces who muster behind Christian Abolition, and they set out in search of the Giant himself. His castle, they find, "stood . . . in the kingdom of Mammon; a large massive edifice flanked it on one side called The State. . . . [This building] was a mixed order of architecture" (p. 55). As the battle-forces draw up for the ensuing combat, it is discovered that the Giant has a brother called Pro-Slavery, who is betrothed to the daughter of Expediency, one False-Charity. This young lady "contended for much meekness towards those who were injuring others," and "never liked to hear the Giant's sins hinted at" (p. 57). As the battle reaches its height,[12] Christian and his companion Constant (a substitute for Faithful) are captured by Pro-Slavery's chief aide, Major Lynch, and thrown into a dungeon similar to the original of Giant Despair. Here they meet a fellow-prisoner, a Negro called White-heart, who becomes their companion for the rest of their journey to the Celestial City. In discussing the war, Christian Abolition suggests that it is actually part of a general border war between the powers of light and darkness, and that it will be extensive (p. 64). "Every pilgrim knows," he says, "that the present war must continue, until one great and final battle takes place in which our prince . . . will appear in person. Then shall he put all enemies under his feet. To that day we look forward with hope" (p. 64). What is merely implied in other American adaptations of *The Pilgrim's Progress,* namely, that the conflagration arising out of the wickedness of slavery is part of the more general pattern of things leading history to the brink of the "time of the end," is here made explicit. There is little doubt that many Calvinist Abolitionists believed in an imminent millennium, and it would seem only natural to them to dramatize the potential conflict between North and South as part of the apocalyptic scheme of history. Purely economic motives, as well as motives of political expediency, are attributed as causes of the war (p. 65). There is no escaping the war: it is an irrepressible conflict, because, as Christian Abolition says, "the road to the Celestial City lies along these borders" (p. 64). Eventually Christian, Constant, and their new companion White-heart escape from Major Lynch's dungeon and proceed on their journey towards the Celestial City. When they encounter incredulous and scoffing wayfarers, such as Prejudice, who never takes a road until he asks "are there any colored people there?" they answer quite simply that "there will be a vast company of [White-heart's] nation" in the Celestial City (p. 81).[13]

Christian and his companions undergo any number of further ordeals on their journey. Vanity Fair, where the pilgrims have gone specifically to warn the inhabitants that the Last Days are approaching, is "at its ripeness, taking its last, worst aspect, a religious shape" (p. 139). The present citizens of the Town of Vanity (like Mr. Humanwise, a student of German theology: "Our best, as well as our most learned men are against you" [p. 158]; and Mr. Worldling, a defender of the world's improvements such as the railroads, steam navigation, "advanced" learning and science) deride the pilgrims, and view with some incredulity these pilgrims who "believed that God . . . God himself—no viceregent—was coming to reign" (p. 154). Eventually Christian is driven out of town, although Constant remains to see what he can do to persuade its citizens of their wickedness. The other pilgrims arrive eventually at the Land of Beulah, after having seen, on the Delectable Mountains, a prospect of the Celestial City "which is soon to come down from God out of heaven" (p. 172). One by one the pilgrims are sent for, to cross the river of death and be met by the angels on the other side. And now, in an interesting innovation on Bunyan's theme, the narrator (dreamer) returns to Vanity Fair, where Constant, at the height of his warfare,[14] has been captured, judged, and is about to be martyred at the stake. Just as his persecutors are about to ignite the first faggot, "an awful light suddenly appears in the East" (p. 186). The Last Days have begun! In a rhetorical and climactic conclusion, the author of *Pilgrim's Progress in the Last Days* affects a tone similar to the ancient psalmists: "Where now," he exclaims, "is the pride of the proud? Where shall guilt hide her millions of slaves?" (p. 186). Constant is raised to his place among the chariots and angels of God, and with the echoes of hallelujah in his ears, the narrator wakes, to pray "Lord, make me valiant for the Truth upon the earth!"

Pilgrim's Progress in the Last Days is a many-sided

document. In the first place, it takes its place beside the hundreds of antislavery tracts which issued from the Abolitionist press in the forties and fifties. Although little known today, this is an absorbing document because it so dramatically predicts the "irrepressible conflict" and condemns slavery as much for its basis in political and economic expediency as because of its inhumanity. Second, it may be regarded as one of the more successful attempts to present the vision of the impending millennium in vivid and dramatic form, and to subordinate all of the elements of attack to the larger notion of the cataclysmic "last days." The year of its publication—1843—was the climactic year for the Millerites. It was also the period during which Hawthorne was most interested in millennial utopias, and during which he wrote most about them; it was also the year in which Bronson Alcott, in a cold and desolated farm at Harvard, Massachusetts—having been deserted by a professed millennialist, Charles Lane—went to bed, turned his face to the wall, refused to eat, and apparently awaited the end of the world. Mrs. Alcott's rescue did not undo the damage to his forsaken Eden, Fruitlands. Finally, *Pilgrim's Progress in the Last Days* is a conspicuous example of the contemporary uses to which Bunyan's *Pilgrim's Progress* was put by latter-day Calvinistic conservatives. Their mistrust of contemporary events allowed them to employ this most familiar allegory as a battle-piece in all-out war in which, as it turned out, they were destined to be defeated.

The California Pilgrim

Christian's journey on foot to the Celestial City was through the wilderness of this world. It is not surprising that, when he reached America, he would walk from the

East towards the western wilderness, arriving eventually in California. Such a scheme would require that the City of Destruction be situated on the east coast, and would allow California to become the New Jerusalem arising out of the wilderness, as in John's apocalyptic prophecy. This is what occurs in Joseph A. Benton's *The California Pilgrim.*[15] The title character, modeled on Bunyan's Christian, becomes discontented with the ease and luxury of the eastern city of Doomsend, where he was born in the early nineteenth century. Eventually, just before a "fiery deluge swept over [Doomsend]," he set out on a "pilgrimage to the west." The final part of his journey to the "land of gold" is by coastal steamer, on which he is accompanied by some fellow-passengers whose previous experiences have convinced them that he will soon abandon his good intentions. They too had once gone on pilgrimage with rules of good living, "and even President Edwards' resolutions in their pockets," but their present disillusionment has convinced them that Californians "were all alike, going in for that which paid the best," and that even "some of the parsons were getting rich" (p. 43). The pilgrim himself is not easily swayed, because his "views of things were governed by President Edwards' resolutions" (p. 14). Having left the City of Destruction in the east to its apocalyptic end, he is now "taking this route through the land of gold, for the golden city, amid the serene mountains in the Glad-land . . ." (p. 14).

Benton's adaptation of Bunyan's *Pilgrim's Progress* to a California gold-rush setting is ingenious, but his story rapidly degenerates into a moralistic tour of the dens of evil around San Fastopolis (San Francisco) and Sloughport (Sacramento), where Benton was pastor of the First Church of Christ. Yet at the same time, the work is interesting because of its implication that California, after a cleansing apocalyptic fire, will grow to become the New Jerusalem. Three years earlier, Benton had delivered a Thanksgiving discourse in Sacramento in which he sketched out the past and present of California and its prospects for the future.[16] The inflated rhetoric of the discourse suggests at what an early date chamber-of-commerce boosterism had ripened in the area, but the image of a new Eden is unmistakable: "A virgin soil of untold richness—elements of vegetable life and growth accumulating for centuries are spread around us. A million of people can not fail to thrive by cultivating the soil—and in fifty years they will be here to make the demonstration. The vine, the fruit tree . . . will flourish. . . . Plants, annual and perennial, esculent roots, melons, maize, wheat, grains of all kinds, will yield returns an hundred fold. . . . What to many an eye seems an arid waste, will blossom in beauty and yield its harvests of joy" (p. 10). Benton sees the discovery of gold as a blessing: "Gold is yet to fill our street—to be as common as in the days of Solomon, and houses of worship in California may yet vie with the temple of Solomon in their costliness, elegance, and the splendor of their decorations" (p. 11). Anticipating Whitman's celebration of the west in "Passage to India,"[17] Benton proclaims that the iron horse "that has drank the waters of the Mississippi," and will now "gladden us in the land whereon the star of empire shall never set" (p. 12), and the telegraph, which, "with its wires of flame, [will] gird all lands and encircle the world," will bring all fame, culture, and advantages to California: "The world's centre will have changed. . . . This will be the land of pilgrimage, and no man will be thought to have seen the world till he has visited California" (p. 12).

Benton did not doubt that the progress of California towards greatness was part of God's plan: "It is not possible that California should not be used in some method, as God's instrument in the progressions of his kingdom. . ." (p. 13), and he viewed California as God's last and noblest creation. Three years later, with the publication of *The California Pilgrim,* Benton's tone of optimism was modified somewhat, and he was far more concerned about the obstacles in the path of progress than with rhetorical prophecies. Nevertheless, there is little question that California will still be the promised land: "During all their pilgrimage, the conviction had grown in their minds, that the land they had journeyed in was the land of all lands, vilify it as men might, and as men would. In due time, they doubted not, it would so appear to all. It only needed better moral influences, and the power of true religion speedily to bring that day" (p. 258).

Benton's sketches of some of the contemporary California types anticipate the writing of young Samuel Clemens, who was soon to arrive upon the scene, and who was to entitle his own first published book "The New Pilgrim's Progress." One of the most engaging characters whom Pilgrim meets is Mr. Doleful Dumps: "[Dumps] . . . had traded largely; and then his customers ran off without paying their debts. He had tried a rancho, but the drouth pinched some of his crops. . . . He had owned a steamboat, and that blew up. He had shipped sand from Gold Bluff, and that did not pay its freight. He had run for office, and got beaten . . ." (pp. 82–83). Another character, Fortunatus Wait—a pseudoscientist—was escorted out of town by a "committee," as he puts it. The ride, he says, was rather a pleasant feature of the affair; but the vehicle they rode him on "was too long and narrow for comfort, with some splinters about it, but nothing to hold on by" (p. 95).

To Benton, and consequently to Pilgrim as he journeys

abroad are also good moralistic Presbyterians, but, far from being regarded with respect, they have become the subject of abusive ridicule.

A Reel in a Bottle, for Jack in the Doldrums

The Reverend George Barrell Cheever, Hawthorne's contemporary at Bowdoin College, rose to national prominence for his dogged and vociferous stand against slavery, but he was well known in his day as a champion of many popular and unpopular causes: he fought for temperance, opposed the removal of the Indians, and condemned the violation of the Sabbath by the railroads.[18] In addition to his lifelong tendency to speak out publicly for what he believed in, Cheever had one central, all-devouring intellectual passion: John Bunyan. Not the least of his own fame was based upon his incredibly popular Bunyan lectures in 1843–44, which were subsequently published and went into many editions in the following two decades.[19] But the *Lectures* represented only the more spectacular aspect of Cheever's obsession. He not only drew upon Bunyan for most of the titles of his own works, but derived many of his themes, sometimes incongruously, from Bunyan's works.[20] Perhaps the most ambitious of Cheever's attempts to make Bunyan speak out against what he considered to be the excesses of a liberal nineteenth century was his allegorical novel, *A Reel in a Bottle, for Jack in the Doldrums.*[21] Judged by any literary standard, *A Reel in a Bottle* could not be called successful, for its effectiveness is severely limited by the frequent and tedious pietistic conversations of the two "pilgrim sailors," Peter and John. Nevertheless, the work bears scrutiny because it is so clearly in the Bunyanesque tradition begun earlier by Weeks and raised to admirable levels by Hawthorne.

As in *The California Pilgrim,* a work published the following year, Cheever placed his pilgrims aboard a ship, rather than on foot, in this case a "grand ship prepared to take passengers across the great sea that lies between us and the Celestial Country" (p. 11). Many persons came down to watch the preparation of the ship (*The Innocents Abroad* begins in much the same way), but few finally chose passage, although there were dire apocalyptic warnings that "their own country was to be visited and burnt up with fire, which would involve the perdition of ungodly men." In Cheever, we meet once again a conservative evangelical theologian who believed in an imminent millennium,[22] and who shared the conventional view that the present population of the ungodly would be destroyed before Christ set up his thousand-year kingdom on earth. Particular victims of his judgment are commercial businessmen (p. 32), modern scientists, especially geologists (p. 46), railroads (p. 52),[23] and mutual insurance companies—not to mention the conventional enemies represented as Deists, Unitarians, Transcendentalists, and "liberal" religious thinkers in general. Cheever's pilgrims have any number of adventures, including a stop at the Country of Hope, located "a great way north," where fugitive slaves are never returned to their masters in the South, and where Satan is characterized as "The Great Slaveholder";[24] an encounter with the ship of Captain Demetrius, who sails from the Country of Gain-is-Godliness, and whose ship barometer "had a trick of stopping at fair weather"; and a layover in the Country of Self-Deceit, where a balloon-riding reviser of the Holy Bible claims that he and his friends are "pretty generally transcendentalizing the whole thing" (p. 41). The most vigorous and extended attack in Cheever's work is reserved for various aspects of "liberal" theology. The pilgrims meet a pleasure yacht skippered by one Captain Glib. The yacht itself was built in the Country of Liberal Christianity; its first mate is named Deism, its helmsman Mr. Man's Wisdom, its second mate Plausible, and its crew made up of men like Surface, Tradition, Anything, and Prejudice. Captain Glib informs the pilgrims that he is "bound now to Cape Transcendental . . . to get the latest notions" (p. 112), and says, "I thank God the world is no longer in leading strings to a squad of Calvinistic theologians" (p. 113). In Cheever's mind the philosophies expressed under the general designations of Deism and Transcendentalism are also responsible for a belief (to his mind a deceptive one) in the idea of Progress. Captain Glib claims that "we . . . by steam navigation, are advancing according to the progressive spirit of the age" (p. 119), and proudly professes his unfaltering belief in the "New Science of the Critical Nineteenth Century" (p. 119). On Captain Glib's ship, so he says, "we belong to the School of Progress" (p. 125). The ultimate destruction of ships like Captain Glib's is of course a certainty. The description of a similar ship encountered by the pilgrims (its skipper is the allegorical counterpart of Apollyon) is typical: "Having been disabled by a shot from the King's ship, she drove on recklessly like a blinded tiger in a burning menagerie, and her shotted guns went off one after another, till at length there was a most awful and magnificent explosion, and for a moment the air was filled with burning, falling fragments, and then all was dark and still" (p. 198). The pilgrims themselves eventually reach the Island of the Communion of Saints (roughly corresponding to Bunyan's Land of Beulah), where life is paradisiacal: "Here were trees, whose fruit was for meat, and the leaves for medicine. Here were orchards of pomegranates . . . spikenard, cinnamon, and all trees of frankincense . . ." (p. 170). At one point in their journey, the pilgrims are treated to a view of "the walls and gates of the New Jerusalem," where "happy beings in white" are continually going in and out (p. 184). Eventually[25] the ship arrives at the gates to the Celestial City, and the pilgrims are observed going up into it.

That *A Reel in a Bottle*—a work now so totally obscure that Cheever's own recent biographer was apparently ignorant of it—could have had such popularity in its own time, going into four or five editions in the 1850's, being republished in England, and ultimately reissued in America in the 1880's, is probably due to three principal reasons. Cheever himself was at the height of his considerable popularity in the period when his work was published: his *Lectures on the "Pilgrim's Progress"* had gone into eight editions by the time *A Reel in a Bottle* was published. In the second place, the general public interest in *The Pilgrim's Progress* was still high. The period of the 1840's, when Cheever and others were capitalizing upon an apparently insatiable public appetite for Bunyan's works, had paved the way for Bunyanesque allegories. In the third place, the controversies between liberal and conservative theology, begun in the earlier part of the century, continued unabated, and Cheever's work represents a strident but unflagging expression of the conservative point of view. In his earlier *Lectures*, Cheever had anticipated certain techniques of criticism which he now employed in *A Reel in a Bottle*.[26] One of these is reminiscent of Hawthorne's treatment of the city of Vanity:

> The town was much altered since Christian and Faithful passed through it, and principally for the reason that a great multitude of pilgrims . . . had concluded . . . that by reason of the increase of refinement and knowledge among the inhabitants, the city itself was very profitable and pleasant to dwell

in, [and had decided] to remain there for an indefinite season, and many of them for the residue of their lives. This began by some of them [taking] part in the purchase and sale of the merchandise of the place, till at length a great part of the business came to be transacted by those who first came to the place in the character of strangers and travellers to the Celestial City. [pp. 238-39]

Cheever's work is pertinent to this study because it is one of a number of works which refashioned Bunyan's *Pilgrim's Progress* into an instrument of satire in order to attack certain "liberal" institutions of the mid-nineteenth century, including deism, unitarianism, transcendentalism, scientism, and progress in general as assumed by these optimistic faiths. Cheever's early reading of Bunyan[27] resulted in a powerful and lifelong influence on his thinking. Everything which he wrote subsequently was saturated with the tone and temper of Bunyan's works, and more than any other American of the period, he attempted to make Bunyan's lessons apply to what in his view was a generation of backsliders.[28]

Modern Pilgrims

George Wood's *Modern Pilgrims,*[29] directly inspired by Hawthorne's "The Celestial Railroad,"[30] is a discursive and often uninspired two-volume novel which takes two fashionable New York couples over Bunyan's route of pilgrimage (although the byways are so extensive as to make the original route unrecognizable). Wood, who was the First General Agent of the Baptist General Tract Society,[31] also was the author of *Peter Schlemiehl in America* and *The Gates Wide Open,* a millennial utopian novel.

Modern Pilgrims follows the pattern established by

earlier works of its type. Written from a narrow point of view, its chief objects of attack include the Roman Catholic Church as well as any kind of doctrine which might be considered in any degree "liberal." Boston Unitarians come in for a major portion of the attack. Narrating the pilgrimage of Mr. and Mrs. (Frank and Gertrude) Trueman and their companions Mr. and Mrs. (Oliver and Annie) Outright, Wood attempts to enlarge upon Hawthorne's themes. New York is the modern City of Destruction, and fashionable New York society, from which the two couples desire to flee, considers it a "special offense" (p. 45) that, at the height of the season, the Truemans and the Outrights should close up one of the "handsomest houses in Fifth Avenue" (p. 46) merely to proceed on a pilgrimage. The couples' own minister, the Episcopalian Dr. Upatree, attempts to dissuade them from a pilgrimage. Upatree is characterized as an imperious religious snob whose prayers were so patronizing that "in his view, the Almighty God was under the highest obligation to him for his condescension" (p. 47).[32] The world of New York's high society (modern Babylon) resembles one which Thorstein Veblen might well have described. In Babylon, the "great mart of commerce, and the monetary centre of the continent" (p. 55), merchant princes had built palaces of red sandstone where they could conspicuously consume their own wealth: "Money, when acquired, must be spent. . . . In spending money lay the touchstone of gentility. . . . The tests of gentility in Babylon were the manner in which the possession of wealth was made manifest in the world; the style of their houses, their furniture, pictures, plate, vases, mirrors, and last, not least, their libraries" (pp. 55–56). Even the churches cannot escape the blight: "Pietism was the rage; and the centres of fashion were the gorgeous, spacious, splendid churches of the Apostolical High Church of Babylon" (p. 57).

Eventually the pilgrims get under way, but like Hawthorne's narrator, they choose to travel by modern conveyances, including railroad trains, rather than on foot. They meet the modern counterpart of Beelzebub, one Count de Ville, who turns out to be a railroad entrepreneur. In his library are many works of theology, but especially evident is his vast collection of the writings of the Jesuit fathers. The principal objects of Wood's attack seem to be Unitarianism, Fourierism, Roman Catholicism, and modernism in general (as exemplified, for instance, in the Women's Rights movement [p. 101]). Significantly, only one pilgrim has actually come on the right path towards the Celestial City, and he came over a "Presbyterian Bridge" (p. 75).[33] The satirical treatment of the various denominations will give an indication of Wood's method. The pilgrims eventually tarry at a number of hotels and way-stations, each of which is obviously representative of some current doctrinal position. These include the *dell' Italia,* "all laid in Roman cement [which] had become petrified" (p. 139); the Old School Hotel (Nassau Hall); the Yale House, "made with the new cement of Mr. Plastic," and all patched up (p. 158); the Wesleyan House, made with a new German cement so that "whatever crevice was stopped up by it was made larger" (p. 160), and the Roger Williams House, where the guests were plain and honest with no style (p. 160).

Wood's methods can be typified in his treatment of the Unitarians. At the Tremont House, the host, Mr. Tollman, (probably Wood's idea of William Ellery Channing), acts as a kind of modern Interpreter. Guests at the Tremont House "really had very vague ideas of the Celestial City, and of what a pilgrimage was designed to be. And yet nothing pleased them so much as being earnest" (p. 129). Mr. Tollman is particularly desirous of "liberalizing" Christian doctrine. He is pleased with the moderate influence his house has exerted over the opinions of "preachers belonging to other houses." "The old fountains of Calvinism," he says, "have been so mixed and altered by artesian wells of limestone we have opened into them, that they are, for the most part, brackish" (p. 108). This was accomplished, boasts Mr. Tollman, "by liberalizing our Christianity" (p. 108).

Modern Pilgrims deserves its present oblivion. It is an endless and disorganized diatribe, and where it is clever, the cleverness is due to the imaginative depth of the two works upon which it sucks like a parasite: Bunyan's *Pilgrim's Progress* and Hawthorne's brief but dramatically effective "The Celestial Railroad." Nevertheless, *Modern Pilgrims* deserved at least cursory scrutiny in this study because it falls into the pattern of a number of books which, with varying degrees of success, attempted to employ Bunyan's allegory as the basis for a satirical onslaught against mid-nineteenth-century theological liberalism.

The five works discussed in the chapter have much in common.[34] One thing which all of them share—I am excluding "The Celestial Railroad"—is a dead level of mediocrity in style. This is undoubtedly one reason why at present they enjoy comparative oblivion. One author during this prewar period, however, rose above the level of mediocrity in his employment of Bunyanesque themes and techniques. This was Hawthorne, and I turn now to a discussion of his works in an attempt to discover in what particular way Bunyan was influential upon them.

III

BUNYAN & HAWTHORNE

MUCK RAKE

THE PILGRIM'S PROGRESS
New York, Tiebout, 1811

Anderson's characteristic signature may be seen in the shadow near Muck Rake's right foot. This familiar representation of Muck Rake is copied from the design of British engraver Thomas Stothard, and may have been in Hawthorne's mind as he drew upon *The Pilgrim's Progress* in portraying Roger Chillingworth in *The Scarlet Letter.*

Chapter Three

NATHANIEL HAWTHORNE once observed that "an American would never understand the passage in Bunyan about Christian and Hopeful going astray along a bypath into the grounds of Giant Despair—from there being no stiles and bypaths in our country."[1] Stiles or not, Hawthorne made ample use of the imagery of footpaths and bypaths in his own works long before he made any overt observation about them. He adapted his pathways to the American landscape as he knew it, and he created his own complex imaginative wilderness, running certain pathways and byways through it.

Christian's famous journey was linear, straight ahead, and on foot. Hawthorne, an inveterate walker himself, but one who feared the tangles and obstacles of underbrush,[2] frequently chose an American wilderness as the setting for important incidents in his works. One might almost say that the center of moral insight in a Hawthorne story is customarily in the middle of the woods. Like the artist in "The Prophetic Pictures," Hawthorne copied natural scenery "as a framework for the delineations of the human form and face instinct with thought, passion, or suffering." The indigenously American wilderness of pines and oaks which appears and reappears so frequently in Hawthorne, becomes important because of the characters who lose their way among the trees, and because of the Eden, utopia, millennium, or Arcadia which these characters invariably search for in its depths.

This chapter is an examination of three primary images in Hawthorne as they appear in a number of his works both early and late. The images—all, I will argue, reflecting Bunyan as a fundamental source—are (1) the disingenuous pilgrim; (2) pathways and byways in a labyrinthine wilderness; (3) the unsuccessful search for the Celestial City. Because these images or themes do not appear separately from each other, I have chosen certain representative works of Hawthorne in which I can demonstrate all of the images at work, namely, *Fanshawe,* "The Celestial Railroad," *The Scarlet Letter,* and *The Blithedale Romance.*

This is not to insist that Hawthorne's work was in some way a feeble American copy of Bunyan, although many examples of such copies, by other authors, exist; it is rather to suggest that an essential allegorical element which can only be called Bunyanesque runs through the center of Hawthorne's work, and illuminates it for those readers who are familiar with Bunyan. As a matter of fact, Hawthorne seems to depend upon one's familiarity with Bunyan in order to reveal, in his own works, pilgrims of an entirely different nature. We find, in Hawthorne, not Bunyan's Christian with his burden, book, and staff, but Bunyan's Ignorance, that "very brisk Lad" who appears walking down a crooked lane leading from the Country of Conceit. We find not Bunyan's "wilderness of this world," but a trackless American forest of puritanical pine trees; and we find, not Bunyan's Celestial City attained, but a millennial New Jerusalem searched for and lost.

Obviously *The Pilgrim's Progress* was not the sole source for Hawthorne's rich imagery of pilgrims, pathways, and paradises lost—one recalls, for example, *The*

Faerie Queene and *The Divine Comedy*, the two other allegories of unquestionable influence upon Hawthorne—but I shall limit myself to those correspondences which appear to be attributable for some special reason to *The Pilgrim's Progress*.[3] Granted that Bunyan's influence upon Hawthorne was pervasive, I hope to demonstrate where Bunyan's work gives particular shape to Hawthorne's.

Fanshawe

Probably one of the reasons why Hawthorne expressed his dissatisfaction with *Fanshawe* and withdrew it after subsidizing its publication was that he recognized that the novel failed in its allegorical intention. The weakness of the book lies not so much in its obvious reliance on the "rant of Neal" and the romantic devices of Walter Scott as in its author's inability to exercise the easy and authoritative control over his material that is so evident in the best of *Twice-Told Tales*. *Fanshawe* interests readers of Hawthorne because in it one may detect its apparent artistic intention, and define thereby its peculiar failure to realize this intention. Norman Holmes Pearson has suggested that when Hawthorne wrote *Fanshawe*, he was "not yet deep enough in the past . . .";[4] actually, it is not so much Hawthorne's later necessity to move deeply into the past which defines the quality of his artistic power, but rather his growing ability to use the materials of a given past to form a convincing imaginative present. Therefore the principal weakness of *Fanshawe* is the attempt and the failure of allegory. The vehicle exists, but is not managed skillfully because it is more Bunyan's than it is Hawthorne's.

Certain images originating in *The Pilgrim's Progress* seem to have given shape to *Fanshawe*. The central motive in the novel—the linear movement along a pathway coupled with a corresponding erratic movement along a bypath—becomes an increasingly important device in Hawthorne's later writing. As in the later stories, the wilderness figures importantly in *Fanshawe* both as setting and as a symbolical device to be manipulated. Physically, the wilderness consists (as it will in his later writing) of a New England forest which is especially abundant in pine growth. It is a woods not unlike the woods near Raymond, Maine, where Hawthorne, *Pilgrim's Progress* in hand, wandered as a boy; the woods around Brunswick, Maine, where he wandered as a college youth; and the woods north of Augusta, Maine, where he visited his friend Horatio Bridge after graduation from Bowdoin. Hawthorne's interest in pine woods was almost an obsession. His recorded descriptions of forests in *The American Notebooks* total thousands of words. Judging from these entries, his attention was particularly caught by tall, bare pines which were left standing among the desolation of less commanding vegetation. Near Augusta he noted "a stately pine, wholly devoid of bark, rising white in aged and stately ruin" (p. 6). Near Pittsfield, he noted "one tall, barkless stem of a tree standing upright, branchless, and with a shattered summit" (p. 63). In the center of that town he noted a ruined elm "of the loftiest and straightest stem that ever I beheld—without a branch or leaf upon it . . ., the top branches, unfortunately, [had] been shattered somehow or other. . . ." In another entry, he describes "the tallest of all the trees, an old, dead, barkless pine, rising white and lonely, though closely surrounded by others; it had been dead for long years . . ." (p. 16). Had these descriptions of trees not been imaginatively developed in Hawthorne's fiction, they might be written off as a kind of curious and wholly unconscious exhibit of

Freudian psychology; as it was, however, Hawthorne's tree-symbolism became important, pervasive, and consistent. The deep woods, when there was no pathway through them, generally represented a condition of moral chaos. Tall old pines within the woods, when they were still living, generally represented the stern and unbending character of the first-generation Puritan settlers; tall old pines which had been long dead, or which had fallen and decayed into mossy stumps, invariably suggest the degradation of the Puritan dogma in generations later than the first. Dorcas, in "Roger Malvin's Burial," sits upon a decayed stump during the tragic climax of that story; the may-pole at Merrymount is a stripped pine; the "tree of death" in "The Gentle Boy" is a mutilated fir situated well off the main track through the forest. Hester Prynne actually sits on a decayed, moss-grown stump at the moment of her most willful act. Pearl sees the old pines as Puritan elders. Zenobia commits suicide under the shadow of an old stump. Examples could be multiplied indefinitely. Hawthorne's personal feeling about forests is expressed in the following notebook entry: "How very desolate looks a forest . . . as if, should you venture one step within its wild, tangled, many-stemmed, and dark-shadowed verge, you would inevitably be lost forever" (p. 31).

Figuratively, the wilderness represents moral chaos and degradation. In *Fanshawe* a single pathway or roadway *through* the wilderness contrasts with byways which lead to death and destruction. Awkward though Hawthorne's management of it is, the image of a straight path (with its corresponding bypaths) is the controlling image in the novel. We see Fanshawe himself descending a hill on the main track through the forest, making "very inconsiderable progress." Ellen, he says, has "arrested" him from continuing a "journey which was likely to prove much longer than he had intended" (p. 11). Life seems to him "but a weary way, without a resting place." Ellen was "formed to walk in the calm and quiet paths of life," but after having rejected the improbable guardianship of Dr. Melmoth, she is compelled to "tread the dark path that lay before her." Her way becomes figuratively and literally dark and intricate as the tale reaches its climax.

An analysis of the climactic scenes in *Fanshawe* will serve to demonstrate not only how consistently Hawthorne developed and relied upon pathway imagery, but also to what degree he was depending upon the basic metaphor of *The Pilgrim's Progress*. Despite its clumsiness, the wilderness scene at the melodramatic conclusion of *Fanshawe* reveals Hawthorne's attempt to allow the conditions of setting and physical action to reinforce the complexity of the moral situation in which the characters are involved. Furthermore, the setting is used in an attempt to dramatize character. It is precisely in their relative positions in the wilderness that Ellen, Butler, and Fanshawe are finally and fully defined.

The scene in which Ellen allows herself to be misguided by Butler into an increasingly "dark and intricate" path has itself involved an ingenious preparation. Her gentle and ineffectual guardian, Dr. Melmoth, who is a slightly diluted eighteenth-century version of a Calvinistic theologian, has created an "artificial wilderness" in his garden, where the sinister villain Butler is able to persuade Ellen that she should trust him and follow him. Dr. Melmoth's garden is actually a brilliant metaphor for his own mind, and it comprises Hawthorne's indictment of post-Puritan Calvinism: "Dr. Melmoth had followed his own fancies in the mode of laying out his garden; and, in consequence, the plan that had undoubtedly existed in his mind was utterly incomprehensible to every one but himself. It was an intermixture of kitchen and flower garden, a labyrinth of winding paths, bordered by hedges, and impeded by shrubbery. Many of the original trees of the forest were still flourishing among the exotics which the doctor had transplanted thither" (p. 20). The bewilderment reflected in Melmoth's labyrinthine garden is repeated as the story reaches its climax, when Ellen is led by Butler away from the main road through the forest into a "devious" and "faintly traced" path overgrown by bushes. Upon descending a steep hill, they come to a stop at the base of a "precipice, so high that the loftiest pine-tops (and many of them seemed to soar to heaven) scarcely surmounted it." This precipice is to become, in many ways, Bunyan's Hill Difficulty transplanted into the heart of the Maine woods:

> The inferior portion of the crag, beneath which Ellen and her guide were standing, varies so far from the perpendicular as not to be inaccessible by a careful footstep. But only one person has been known to attempt the ascent of the superior half, and only one the descent; yet, steep as is the height, trees and bushes of various kinds have clung to the rock, where-ever their roots could gain the slightest hold; thus seeming to prefer the scanty and difficult nourishment of the cliff to a more luxurious life in the rich interval that extends from its base to the river. [pp. 66-67]

The original Hill Difficulty had a spring, not a river, at its base, and "there were also in the same place two other ways besides that which came straight from the gate; one turned to the left hand, and the other to the right, at the bottom of the hill; but the narrow way lay right up the hill, and the name of the going up the side of the hill is called Difficulty."[5] Christian's companions at the foot of the Hill Difficulty were Formalist and Hypocrisy. Deciding to avoid the hill, Formalist went down one of the byways "called Danger, which led into a great wood"; Hypocrisy "took directly up the way to Destruction, which led him into a wide field, full of dark mountains, where he stumbled and fell, and rose no more" (p. 104). Hawthorne's tale has allowed for the same pattern of events: Dr. Melmoth, with his artificial wilderness, is like Formalist in creating a great wood for himself; Butler, the obvious hypocrite, resembles Hypocrisy even to his stumbling, falling, and rising no more, as we shall see in a moment. Other details of Hawthorne's hill in *Fanshawe* resemble those of the original Hill Difficulty. Corresponding to the arbor "midway to the top of the hill" in *The Pilgrim's Progress* is Hawthorne's somewhat more sublime "cave": "Just at the termination of the accessible portion of the crag, [the birch and 'funereal' pines] are so numerous, and their foliage so dense, that they completely shroud from view a considerable excavation, formed, probably, hundreds of years since . . ." (p. 67). Hawthorne's "arbor," where Butler leaves Ellen alone, is "the ultimate point where mortal footsteps may safely tread." Ellen's predicament recalls Christian's. Deserted by Formalist and Hypocrisy, Christian rested from his arduous, brief clambering, fell asleep, and let his precious roll fall out of his hand. Awakening from his slumber, he proceeded without the roll, but met dangers and terrors against which he was now helpless to protect himself. Ellen almost falls into a "dreamless slumber," but rouses herself by noticing the details of the cave: "She now perceived, wherever the smooth rock afforded place for them, the initials, or the full-length names of former visitants of the cave. What wanderer on mountain-tops or in deep solitudes has not felt the influence of these records of humanity, telling him, when such a conviction is soothing to his heart, that he is not alone in the world?" (p. 69). Gaining new courage, yet entirely without protection, Ellen leaves the cave and proceeds alone along the bypath. But, like Christian without his protective roll, she is now terrified by "Nature in her wildest forms." Her path is a descent.

At the very base of the cliff, Ellen arrives at the extremities of her mental and moral bewilderment. Now she realizes that her guide is false, "that danger was at hand, and that, in the deep wilderness, there was none to help her, except that Being with whose inscrutable purposes it might consist to allow the wicked to triumph for a season, and the innocent to be brought low" (p. 69). In *The Scarlet Letter* and *The Blithedale Romance* Hawthorne was to repeat the theme of an essentially good but innocent person being falsely guided by a stronger person into the bewildering labyrinths of a wilderness, but when he wrote *Fanshawe,* his control of such themes was not fully within his power.

Even the awkwardness and the melodrama of the ensuing scene, however, did not entirely defeat Hawthorne's intention of making his landscape serve the multiple purpose of romantic suspense, moral analogy, and literary allusion. While Butler prepares to attack the helpless girl at the cliff-base, Fanshawe is searching for her. Forced to follow "the narrow and winding path," he is soon "desperately bewildered"; his "way" is "frequently interrupted by rocks, that thrust their huge gray heads from the ground, compelling him to turn aside." Finally he arrives at the top of the cliff, where he stands "gazing down where the sunbeams slept so pleasantly at the roots of the tall old trees, with whose highest tops he was upon a level" (p. 74).[6] Butler, disturbed in his criminal act, looks up to the top of the cliff; Fanshawe appears as an all-judging divinity: "There was something awful, to [Butler's] apprehension, in the slight form that stood so far above him, like a being from another sphere, looking down upon his wickedness" (p. 74). Angered at Fanshawe's discovery and intrusion, he begins "a desperate attempt to ascend the cliff." But it must be recalled that "only one person [had] been known to attempt the ascent of the superior half . . ." of the cliff. Butler clambers up the cliff like a thwarted "Christian": "The space which only had hitherto been deemed accessible was quickly passed; and in a moment more he was half-way up the precipice, clinging to trees, shrubs, and projecting portions of the rock, and escaping through hazards which seemed to menace inevitable destruction" (p. 75). Fanshawe watches "his upward progress, [thinking] that every step would be his last." It is the Difficult Hill which defeats the hypocrite, not Fanshawe: "When within a few feet of the summit, the adventurer grasped at a twig too slenderly rooted to sustain his weight. It gave way in his hand, and he fell backward down the precipice. His head struck against the less perpendicular part of the rock, whence the body rolled heavily down to the detached fragment, of which mention has heretofore been made. There was no life left in him. With all the passions of hell alive in his heart, he had met the fate that he intended for Fanshawe" (p. 75).

It would be premature to conclude that Fanshawe, perched safely at the summit of the Difficult Hill, is more like Bunyan's Christian than is the unfortunate Butler. In a brief and unconsciously symbolic ceremony of baptism, Fanshawe guides Ellen into her new life, but the new guide suffers from subtle defects of his own. Fanshawe's loneliness is not like Christian's, but is rather the result of his self-imposed intellectual isolation. His eagerness for knowledge is clearly dangerous and, as in the case of Nathanael Mather to whom he is compared, leads to his early death. Fanshawe rejects Ellen's offer to be *his* guide (p. 79), and when we realize that Ellen clearly represents *faith,* we see how *Fanshawe* anticipates "Young Goodman Brown."

Fanshawe is the first of a number of Hawthorne's intellectual heroes whose "proud and lonely thoughts" led them away from the salvation offered by "the quiet paths" (p. 79). A pattern has been established, and Hawthorne's later heroes will invariably choose bypaths in their lonely, intellectual, and futile search for the Holy City in the American wilderness.

Hawthorne's failure in *Fanshawe* results from his attempt to use as pure allegory the rhetorical and artificial materials at his command. Because the materials were not yet his own, the result was improbable and melodramatic. In later works, Bunyan's allegorical vehicle will be "absorbed" into Hawthorne's "realistic" material, and the result will be more satisfactory. Gray rocks obstructing the progress of misguided pilgrims, puritanical pine trees with their roots in darkness and their tops swaying crazily in the bright sun, and pathways through a bewildering wilderness will be employed more subtly and less melodramatically. But the importance of such devices as these to Hawthorne's later work lies in the fact that they were first experimentally developed in *Fanshawe,* and it would appear that the essential imagery of *The Pilgrim's Progress* lent itself to the experiment.

"THE CELESTIAL RAILROAD"

The four years 1842–1846 were crucially important for Hawthorne as an individual and as a writer. They marked his beginning happiness as a husband and father. They occurred at the conclusion of his ill-fated experience at Brook Farm, and they span a period during which he searched to link the real world of his contemporary experience with the romantic world of his imagination.[7] Hawthorne's concern, in his major American romances, with disingenuous reformers and their utopias of one sort or another, is prefigured at this time by a series of sketches in which whole worlds of reformers are destroyed by apocalyptic fires. If the mature romances betray a latent sympathy for Dimmesdale and his hope for a New Jerusalem, Holgrave and his wish for a new Eden, and Coverdale in his wavering position at Blithedale, this earlier period reveals only a symbolic sweeping away of reform and reformers: the world purified in preparation for a new Adam and Eve.

The period of these four years was spent comfortably in the Old Manse in Concord. The abode offered as much isolation from society as Hawthorne, always a solitary individual, needed at the time, and his bride relished the opportunity to screen her lover from his admirers while herself sharing the entire intimacy of his companionship. It is not surprising, under these circumstances, that the new couple would think of themselves as Adam and Eve,[8] or that the young husband would attempt a sketch in which a new Adam and Eve found themselves abroad in a civilization swept clear of people. "The New Adam and Eve," however, has more in common with the other sketches written during this period than the superficial fact that it was composed in the Old Manse. Three themes prevail in the sketches: the theme of innocence or Eden already mentioned; the theme of hopelessly deluded visionaries; and the eschatological theme. The early 1840's, in fact, might be labeled with impunity the "Day of

Doom" phase of Hawthorne's development, for the destruction, often by fire, of his contemporary world is a recurrent image and becomes a principal theme. "Fire Worship," for example, establishes a tone, sustained in the following sketches, of reverence for open fire as a destroyer. The worlds to be consumed are subsequently delineated in "The Hall of Fantasy" (full of "noted reformers of the day"), doomed when William Miller's prophecy is realized; "The Procession of Life," built upon a Doomsday image; "The New Adam and Eve"; "Earth's Holocaust"; and "The Celestial Railroad." In these sketches Hawthorne seems to have been struggling to abandon one imaginary cosmos in order to enter a new one. What he destroys, it must be emphasized, is a special world inhabited by eccentrics, visionaries, misguided prophets, and reformers. Hawthorne's struggle during this period results in a clarification of his ultimate distinction between the real world of his contemporary experience and the romantic world of the imagination. A persistent image in Hawthorne, that of the isolated individual who would, by one plunge as it were, immerse himself into the activities of his contemporaries, reflects the young author's state of mind during the Old Manse period. Genuinely distressed by his experience at Brook Farm, where he could not compose and milk cows at the same time, he was nevertheless unprepared to relinquish entirely his loyalty to his fellow reformers. A comparison of the introductions to *Mosses* and *The Scarlet Letter* suggests that whereas the *Mosses* introduction is openly apologetic for being intrusively personal and bears only indirectly upon the sketches which follow it, the later "Custom House" sketch, while reflecting the identical problem of "a more personal relation with the public," allows for a framework and a transition to the past in which the story is set.[9]

Hawthorne's disenchantment with Brook Farm had been painful, and though he and Sophia entertained visitors from the farm at the Old Manse, the images in the sketches written during the period point to an ultimate reaction against their notions. In the winter of 1845 Nathaniel and Sophia read Fourier in order to understand the conversion of Brook Farm to Associationism. Their response was violently negative.[10]

It was during this period, and as a result of the forces I have described, that there emerged in Hawthorne's work a characteristic figure: the visionary pilgrim who is in fact deluded in his quest for the Celestial City. The popularity of William Miller's theories in the early 1840's would not have been the only reason why Hawthorne would refer to him repeatedly in the sketches. Brook Farm itself had been guided by George Ripley's faith in an imminent millennium.[11] The prototype, therefore, in many ways, of Hawthorne's later self-deluded visionaries is the figure of the narrator in "The Celestial Railroad," unquestionably one of the most successful sketches of the group written during this period.

The story takes its cue from earlier American adaptations of Bunyan's *Pilgrim's Progress,* and relies for its success upon the reader's familiarity with the original work. The narrator, or dreamer, unlike his counterpart in Bunyan's allegory, is himself on pilgrimage. Here it is the wealthy and fashionable who are pilgrims, and they ride to the Celestial City on a railroad train whose engineer is a fiery Apollyon. Their burdens are conveniently loaded into a baggage car; the Hill Difficulty is avoided by means of a tunnel; and Pope-and-Pagan's cavern is now occupied by the Giant Transcendentalist. The narrator and the other railroad passengers are eventually to be conveyed to their everlasting destruction on a terrifying ferryboat.

Hawthorne's travesty is, like other American "Pilgrim's Progresses" of the period, a satirical indictment of modernism and "reform" in their many guises. Religious liberalism is attacked through the treatment of the vain and superficial optimism in the cathedrals in the new City of Vanity. Faith in mechanical and scientific progress is satirized through the symbol of the railroad train. The present generation, in sum, has lost that deep insight into the human condition represented in Bunyan's work by the Slough of Despond, the Hill Difficulty, and the Man in the Iron Cage. But the splendid success of "The Celestial Railroad" depends ultimately upon Hawthorne's ingenious distortion of the narrator-pilgrim himself, for it would be obvious to any reader familiar with Bunyan that the narrator is not Christian—Bunyan's plodding, plain man—but Ignorance, his erstwhile traveling-companion. The original Ignorance was characterized by his self-confident but obviously uninformed optimism. He thinks he will get in at the gate to the Celestial City because he knows God's will, has "been a good liver, [and paid] every man his own." Ignorance admonishes Christian and Hopeful to "be content to follow the religion of [their own] country, and [he] will follow the religion of [his]." Bunyan's seventeenth-century Ignorance is peculiarly "modern" in that he believes that Christ's atonement justified all men for all time, that no sense of one's own depravity is necessary for salvation, and that divine revelation is based upon silly superstition. His counterpart in "The Celestial Railroad" fails to listen to good counsel, is charmed by the easy way to heaven represented by the burdenless railroad and the sophisticated church-doctrines of Vanity-Fair, and spurns the harsher realities of the genuine pilgrimage. The narrator is, in other words, a disingenuous pilgrim lacking the proper credentials, and he will reappear in different "veils" in the later romances: as Dimmesdale in *The Scarlet Letter,* as Coverdale in *The Blithedale Romance,* and as Clifford in *The House of the Seven Gables.*

By allowing all of the passengers to be carried to their own destruction, and by implying the comparable demise of the citizens of Vanity, Hawthorne underscored his indictment of the shallow liberalism of his own generation. Although it is neither the first nor the most extensive of the American "Pilgrim's Progresses" written to satirize the shallowness of nineteenth-century "progress," "The Celestial Railroad" is undoubtedly the least tedious, succeeding in its brevity where numerous similar works failed. Hawthorne's sketch should be recognized, however, not for its originality, but for the place it shared with similar Bunyan adaptations in championing a mid-century conservative point of view. Its suspicions are the common property of the other American adaptations of *The Pilgrim's Progress,* as are the grounds for its judgments against modernism. The primary importance of "The Celestial Railroad" as a measure of Hawthorne's own development as a writer is that it gave him the identity of a hero he was to use, with variation, again and again. That hero is not Bunyan's Christian; he is Bunyan's Ignorance, and he strides, or falters, in the later romances, along the pathways of a wilderness he scarcely understands.

The Scarlet Letter

The Scarlet Letter may be regarded as a legend about the progress of some pilgrims in New England, and we may learn much about the intention of the novel by examining the pathways and byways taken by its pilgrims. The principal characters are defined with respect to the way in which they walk and the pathways they choose or avoid. Furthermore, the dramatic intensity of the story often depends upon the imagery of walking: climactic chapters, such as "A Forest Walk" and "The Procession" carry this theme to its limits. We may take the relationship between Christian's journey on foot from the City of Destruction to the Celestial City, and the paths taken by Hester, Dimmesdale, and Chillingworth, as more than coincidental, for Hawthorne refers to Bunyan directly and indirectly. But it would be a mistake to search for specific parallels between *The Pilgrim's Progress* and *The Scarlet Letter*: Hawthorne was not writing an allegory of an allegory.

Much of the action in *The Scarlet Letter* occurs, as it were, on foot. Roger Chillingworth, for example, is first seen standing on the edge of a crowd (also standing), "clad in a strange disarray of civilized and savage costume" (p. 119). He has emerged from a foot-journey through the wilderness, and he describes himself as a "wanderer, sorely against [his] will" (p. 120). Originally from a city (Amsterdam), he has undergone a transformation—a kind of unholy rebirth—in his journey from the city into the wilderness, where he learned the black art of the forest savages. "What could he, whose sphere was in great cities, be seeking in the wilderness?" (p. 155). He is a crooked wanderer among crooked bypaths: "So Roger Chillingworth—a deformed old figure . . . took leave of Hester Prynne, and went stooping away along the earth. He gathered here and there an herb, or grubbed up a root, and put it into the basket on his arm. His gray beard almost touched the ground, as he crept onward. Hester gazed after him a little while, looking with a half-fantastic curiosity to see whether the tender grass of early spring would not be blighted beneath him, and show the wavering track of his footsteps . . ." (pp. 187–88).[12] The extraordinary similarity between this physical description of Roger Chillingworth and the most frequently reproduced picture of Muck-rake would encourage speculation that Hawthorne derived his description of Chillingworth from it. Not only is Chillingworth physically like Muck-rake (as characteristically illustrated), but spiritually also.

Just as Chillingworth is defined more clearly for us because we observe him on his walks around the fringes of the settlement—a stooping, grubbing, wavering old man, so, too, the other characters. Pearl cannot walk a straight path; she ambles, scurries, scampers, halts; her gait is always uneven, and hers is a "zigzag course" (p. 229). Dimmesdale, too, reminds the reader of Bunyan's familiar emphasis upon the dangers of byways. He is described as ". . . a being who felt himself quite astray and at a loss in the pathway of human existence, and could only be at ease in some seclusion of his own. Therefore, so far as his duties would permit, he trod in the shadowy bypaths . . ." (p. 123).[13] But with him the matter is more complex. Arthur Dimmesdale, regarded as a pilgrim (his own term for himself [p. 169]), is a thwarted "Christian," a sort of combination of Pliable, Christian, and Ignorance. Like Pliable, he is easily persuaded to begin his pilgrimage, but he is easily tempted down bypaths. Like Ignorance, he believes he is on the right road to the Celestial City, although he is obviously not.

Dimmesdale's likeness to Ignorance requires a closer look at *The Pilgrim's Progress.* At the close of Part I of Bunyan's allegory, the Dreamer, or Narrator, has watched Christian and Hopeful cross the river where they are met by the two ministering angels, and enter into the gates of the Celestial City; their erstwhile companion, Ignorance, now captures his attention: "Now while I was gazing upon all these things, I turned my head to look back, and saw Ignorance come up to the river side; but he soon got over, and that without half the difficulty which the other two men met with. For it happened that there was then in that place, one Vain-hope, a ferryman, that with his boat helped him over. . . ."[14] Ignorance is met by the two angels, who demand of him his certificate of entrance: "So he fumbled in his bosom for one,[15] and found none. Then said they, Have you none? But the man answered never a word. So they told the King, but he would not come down to see him, but commanded the two Shining Ones that conducted Christian and Hopeful to the City, to go out and take Ignorance, and bind him hand and foot, and have him away. Then they took him up, and carried him through the air, to the door that I saw in the side of the hill, and put him in there. Then I saw that there was a way to hell, even from the gates of Heaven, as well as from the City of Destruction! So I awoke, and behold it was a dream" (p. 166).[16] The details of the foregoing passage become important for *The Scarlet Letter.* In Chapter X, "The Leech and his Patient," Hawthorne describes the light which gleamed from Chillingworth's eyes: "Sometimes a light glimmered out of the physician's eyes, burning blue and ominous, like the reflection of a furnace, or, let us say, like one of those gleams of ghastly fire that darted from Bunyan's awful doorway in the hill-side, and quivered on the pilgrim's face. The soil where this dark miner was working had perchance shown indications that encouraged him" (p. 160). The meaning of the reference would have been obvious to Hawthorne's readers, familiar as they were with *The Pilgrim's Progress.* Dimmesdale, the pilgrim, resembles Ignorance to the degree that Chillingworth is able to exert an influence upon him; thus the gleam from the physician's eyes falls upon pilgrim Dimmesdale in the same way that the gleams of fire from Bunyan's awful doorway in the hillside fall upon Ignorance just before he is cast into the fire. No wonder Arthur Dimmesdale's hand is so often fumbling in his bosom.

The association becomes even more decisive when we examine Dimmesdale's behavior as the action reaches its climax. The minister had been on a specific mission when Hester called him aside from the main track through the forest into an area of confused, labyrinthine wilderness: he had been to pay a visit to the celebrated "Apostle to the Indians," the Reverend John Eliot. Hawthorne, a deep student of early colonial history, was specifically aware of the fact that Eliot conceived of his peculiar mission as a millennial one.[17] Thus it is upon his return from a talk with an unconventional Puritan divine whose schemes are radically Utopian, that Dimmesdale is attracted into a pathless wilderness by Hester's call. To this point in the story Dimmesdale has been weighted with a distinct burden: "To the high mountain-peaks of faith and sanctity he would have climbed, had not the tendency been thwarted by the burden, whatever it might be, of crime or anguish, beneath which it was his doom to totter" (p. 168). Hawthorne adds that it was "this very burden . . . that gave him sympathies so intimate with the sinful brotherhood of mankind" (p. 168). Dimmesdale's burden, unlike Christian's, is not cast off early in his pilgrimage: "More than once he had cleared his throat, and drawn in the long, deep, and tremulous breath, which, when sent forth again, would come burdened with the black secret of his soul" (p. 169). But the circumstances of Dimmesdale's unburdening in the forest, when it occurs, are even more decidedly different from Christian's. It is Hester, not God's ministering angels, who accosts the tottering and hesitant pilgrim, and she hails him from a position well off the path:

When her elf-child had departed, Hester Prynne made a step or two towards the track that led through the forest, but still remained under the deep shadow of the trees. She beheld the minister advancing along the path, entirely alone, and leaning on a staff which he had cut by the wayside. He looked haggard and feeble, and betrayed a nervous despondency in his air, which had never so remarkably characterized him in his walks about the settlement, nor in any other situation where he deemed himself liable to notice. . . . There was a listlessness in his gait; as if he saw no reason for taking one step further, nor felt any desire to do so, but would have been glad . . . to fling himself down at the root of the nearest tree, and lie there passive, for evermore. [p. 195]

Hester now persuades Arthur to flee with her from the restrictions imposed by the New England community; the ultimate choice they make for a place of refuge is significantly the cities of Europe. There are no Vanity Fairs in Puritan New England.

Before we examine Dimmesdale's behavior following his decision to flee, we must examine Hester's part in the action. Hester, almost always presented to us in isolation, is seen most characteristically as a lonely wanderer, "walking to and fro, with those lonely footsteps, in the little world with which she was outwardly connected." After the publicity of her crime, she has "the passes of the dark, inscrutable forest open to her," and these bypaths match and encourage "the wildness of her nature." In some ways, her scarlet letter becomes a kind of burning lantern in the darkness, its function to light up the pathway for other pilgrims. In ironic contrast, Dimmesdale, in his public sermons, expresses the wish to be the light which will aid his fellow-pilgrims along the pathway

shame and anguish departed from her spirit. Oh exquisite relief! She had not known the weight, until she felt the freedom!" (p. 204).

Not content like Christian to wait patiently until they come to the place of deliverance, where the burdens will fall off by themselves, Hester and Arthur, acting upon an impulse toward unconstrained freedom bred in the chaos of the wilderness, cast off their burdens prematurely. They must pay the consequences. Earlier in the tale, Hester recognized that "there is no path to guide us out of this dismal maze," and she saw herself, Chillingworth, and Dimmesdale as "here wandering together in this gloomy maze of evil, and stumbling, at every step, over the guilt wherewith we have strewn our path." But she is not content, like Chillingworth, to conclude that "it has all been a dark necessity" (p. 187). Now the apparent simplicity of her plan of escape blinds her to all the intricacies of guilt which earlier were clear to her.[18] The effect of decision upon Dimmesdale is remarkable. Having decided that "the Old World, with its crowds and cities, offered a more eligible shelter and concealment than the wilds of New England, or all America," he leaves Hester and Pearl in the forest to return to the settlement in order to write his Election Sermon, which will be his last. The description of his return through the forest is an indication of the hold upon Hawthorne's imagination which *The Pilgrim's Progress* maintained, for now the "Christian pilgrim," having prematurely cast off his burden, finds the going easy. There is no Hill Difficulty to climb, no Slough of Despond to struggle through. Dimmesdale is once more like Pliable, who had become angered at his slow progress in the Slough of Despond: "May I get out again with my life, you shall possess the brave country alone for me. And, with that, he gave a desperate struggle or two, and got out of the mire on that side of the slough which was next to his own house: so away he went, and Christian saw him no more."[19]

The dominant feeling of a sinner on the "City of Destruction" side of the Slough of Despond, who seems to have escaped from it, will be elation, and this is Dimmesdale's mental state for twenty-four hours. As he returns out of the forest, the world looks decidedly easier to live in:

The excitement of Mr. Dimmesdale's feelings, as he returned from his interview with Hester, lent him unaccustomed physical energy, and hurried him townward at a rapid pace. The pathway among the woods seemed wilder, more uncouth with its rude natural obstacles, and less trodden by the foot of man, than he remembered it on his outward journey. But he leaped across the plashy places, thrust himself through the clinging underbrush, climbed the ascent, plunged into the hollow, and overcame, in short, all the difficulties of the track, with an unweariable activity that astonished him. He could not but recall how feebly, and with what frequent pauses for breath, he had toiled over the same ground, only two days before. [p. 212]

The minister's return to town is accompanied by temptations to "strange and wicked eccentricities" (p. 216). He wants to tell dirty stories to children, he exchanges curses with a drunken seaman, and he shows undue respect to witch-like old Mistress Hibbins. He regards himself as a new man, having left his former self "yonder in the forest . . . by a mossy tree-trunk" (p. 213),[20] and he "fancies himself inspired" as he sets about rewriting his Election Sermon. Dimmesdale's rebirth, like Chillingworth's, is an ironic distortion: it lacks the sanction of divine salvation. Unlike Christian, this pilgrim listened to perverse interpreters and disburdened himself prematurely. The product of his unnaturally heightened sensibility is a "new" Election Sermon which takes the millennium as its subject and prophesies that the New Jerusalem may be established in New England. Dimmesdale's visit with John Eliot, immediately before his momentous interview with Hester in the forest bypath, indicates the probable source of his millennial inspiration. Eliot, a Fifth-Monarchy man, believed that the conversion of the savages—the lost Ten Tribes—was necessary before the New Jerusalem could be built.[21] When Roger Chillingworth steps in to ask Dimmesdale how he found "that godly man, the Apostle Eliot," he also brings up the question of the unfinished Election Sermon. As he leaves the minister, he remarks knowingly that "a good man's prayers are golden recompense," and comprise the "current gold coin of the New Jerusalem." It is no surprise, therefore, to find that Dimmesdale's new sermon, written under the spell of his distorted rebirth, takes the subject it does:

> His subject, it appeared, had been the relation between the Deity and the communities of mankind, with a special reference to the New England which they were here planting in the wilderness. And, as he drew towards the close, a spirit of prophecy had come upon him, constraining him to its purpose as mightily as the old prophets of Israel were constrained; only with this difference, that, whereas the Jewish seers had denounced judgments and ruin on their country, it was his mission to foretell a high and glorious destiny for the newly gathered people of the Lord. [p. 231]

As Dimmesdale delivers his prophetically inspired sermon, Hester, in the market place, learns that Chillingworth will be aboard the escape ship—the Spanish buccaneer vessel whose captain resembles the ferryman Vain-hope in *The Pilgrim's Progress*. As she realized their predicament, Hester's ". . . steadfastly enduring spirit almost sank, at last, on beholding this dark and grim countenance of an inevitable doom, which—at the moment when a passage seemed open for the minister and herself out of their labyrinth of misery—showed itself, with an unrelenting smile, right in the midst of their path" (p. 230).

The final scaffold scene depends for its effect upon the contrast between "the sainted minister in the church," and the "woman of the scarlet letter in the market-place." Dimmesdale, who, while he delivers his Election Sermon, reaches, in the eyes of the community, "the very proudest eminence of superiority," is contrasted with Hester, who "stood in [a] magic circle of ignominy." But the contrast is not only between Dimmesdale in his position and Hester in hers: it is also between Dimmesdale's earlier false unburdening and his final climactic true unburdening.

The procession of "venerable and majestic fathers" makes a broad pathway through the people, who withdraw reverently to let them pass. Dimmesdale's spiritual progress, however, is only possible at the expense of halting the procession. Only when it comes to a complete stop does the almost lifeless minister, tottering under his heavy burden of guilt, make his final confession and revelation, and thus find relief. The triumph of the unburdening at the scaffold, in contrast with the earlier unburdening in the forest, lies in the fact that the people are now touched in an honest and human way: "[Their] great heart was thoroughly appalled, yet overflowing with tearful sympathy, as knowing that some deep life-matter—which, if full of sin, was full of anguish and repentance likewise—was now to be laid open to them" (p. 234). Roger Chillingworth is now powerless to harm his patient. The description of Dimmesdale's final minutes is absorbing: "There was a sweet and gentle smile over his face, as of a spirit sinking into deep repose; nay, now that the burden was removed, it seemed almost as if he would be sportive with the child,—'dear little Pearl, wilt thou kiss me now? Thou wouldst not, yonder, in the forest! But now thou wilt?' Pearl kissed his lips. A spell was broken."

Despite the intentional ambiguity surrounding the events following Dimmesdale's death, we must examine, in the light of this view of Dimmesdale as a latter-day unburdened "Christian," the progress of Hester and Pearl. Hester is temperamentally incapable of remaining in Europe (the City of Destruction) and she returns appropriately to her old paths to "[take] up her long-forgotten shame." Pearl, on the contrary, becomes a woman of the world. Her father, at his death, predicted that she would not "forever do battle with the world, but be a woman in it" (p. 236). Thus it is ironic that Pearl fulfills his prediction in a manner not intended by him, when she inherits Chillingworth's fortune, becomes "the richest heiress of her day, in the New World," chooses to remain in Europe, and associates her destiny with mysterious and alien nobility. The full power of the final passage of *The Scarlet Letter* is best felt when we recall that Pearl's letters from Europe "came, with armorial seals upon them, though of bearings unknown to English heraldry." Pearl's chosen life is clearly not the life of a Pilgrim. It is one of "comfort and luxury," in marked contrast to the austere simplicity of her mother's life. Surrounding Hester's grave "there were monuments carved with armorial bearings; and on this simple slab of slate . . . there appeared the semblance of an engraved escutcheon. It bore a device, a herald's wording of which might serve for a motto and a brief description of our now concluded legend; so sombre is it, and relieved only by one ever-glowing point of light gloomier than the shadow:—'ON A FIELD, SABLE, THE LETTER A, GULES.'" The pilgrimage legend is finished as if not to be again repeated in history.

Hawthorne drew upon *The Pilgrim's Progress* both for thematic material and for character portrayal. The primary figure of the most famous prose allegory of modern literature was a burdened Christian pilgrim making his solitary way on foot through a wilderness from the City of Destruction to the Celestial City, confronted at crucial points by the external adversary of a deformed monster, Apollyon, and by the internal consuming burden of despair. In *The Scarlet Letter* the allegorical setting of the New England colony is the wilderness of this world, flanked on the one side by the City of Destruction (Europe), and on the other by the dark chaos of the primeval forest. Dimmesdale is a burdened "Christian" who combines in his character the weakness of Pliable and the gullibility of Ignorance, but who, like Christian, despite his temptations away from the straight path into the bypaths of the wilderness, ultimately is relieved of his external and internal burdens. Hawthorne was obviously not trying to rewrite *The Pilgrim's Progress,* as he had done in "The Celestial Railroad," but it would seem that the allegorical profundity of Bunyan's classic indirectly gave shape and significance to Hawthorne's allegory of a New England pilgrimage.

The Blithedale Romance

Recent critical estimates of *The Blithedale Romance* have suggested a complexity of characterization in the novel, especially with regard to the role of Miles Coverdale, whose limitations as a narrator, hitherto ascribed to Hawthorne, are understood to be Coverdale's alone.[22] Such a reading of *The Blithedale Romance* reinforces the idea that the novel, far from suffering the limitations suspected of it by earlier critics, represents one of Hawthorne's most successful artistic achievements.

What I wish to propose here is that characterization in *The Blithedale Romance* echoes that in *The Pilgrim's Progress.* Bunyan's influence upon *The Blithedale Romance* is pervasive, although indirect. Of course, Hawthorne refers directly to *The Pilgrim's Progress* in connection with the character of Hollingsworth, but more important than this is the fact that the models for the principal characters in *The Blithedale Romance* seem to have originated, at least in part, from the relationships which exist between the characters in the Second Part of *The Pilgrim's Progress.*[23] The imaginative prototype for Hollingsworth is Great-heart—the guide, spiritual adviser, and protector of Christiana and Mercy. The prototype for Priscilla in *The Blithedale Romance* is Mercy—the faint, gentle seamstress who becomes Christiana's devoted servant-companion. In a very general sense, Christiana herself is the prototype for Zenobia: both women are without fathers and husbands; both women have been deserted by their husbands at some earlier period; both women are in search of either a father or a husband; both women are inspired by "dreams and visions" to engage upon spiritual quests which seem ridiculous to their neighbors; both women involuntarily find themselves accompanied by a physically weak but spiritually compatible maidservant; and both women rely for protection, comfort, and spiritual direction upon a great, shaggy, fatherly man. Christiana, of course, ultimately bids good-by to Great-heart and crosses the River of Death, where presumably she is rewarded by being reunited with Christian in the Celestial City. Zenobia's prospective reward, after she crosses what Hollingsworth describes as the "Black River of Death," is somewhat less certainly attractive.

But the differences between characters in the two works are as important as the similarities. Whereas Christiana's husband deserted her for the devout purpose of proceeding on a pilgrimage, Zenobia's husband (if we are to presume that she had one) was a scoundrel, and left her because he disapproved of her charity to the poor. Christiana, furthermore, was left with four children; Zenobia, although so remarkably ripe, is conspicuously childless.

But before we pursue further the relationship between Christiana and Zenobia, we must turn to the similarities between Mercy and Hawthorne's Priscilla, some of which are indeed striking. In the first place, both girls are good but timid followers. Priscilla is a "pale, western child," a "tremulous little creature, shrinking involuntarily from all mankind, but in timidity, and no [sic] sour repugnance. There was a lack of human substance in her . . ." (p. 548). Mercy is likewise a timid little creature. She comes along with Mrs. Timorous out of curiosity to examine Christiana and to dissuade her from going on a pilgrimage, but something about Christiana fascinates her, and when Mrs. Timorous is ready to return to town, Mercy will not go with her: "Mercy was at a stand, and could not readily comply with her neighbor; and that for a two-fold reason.—1st. Her bowels yearned over Christiana . . . 2dly. Her bowels yearned over her own soul; for what Christiana had said, had taken some hold upon her mind."[24] Mercy, on bidding Mrs. Timorous leave without her, decides "to walk this sunshine morning a little way with [Christiana]" (p. 176). When Priscilla is carried to Blithedale by Hollingsworth, Zenobia regards the little creature with marked coldness, but agrees that the girl can probably be of some use to the community. (Priscilla is a seamstress whose skill in making curious little cloth purses and small articles of clothing will be of some benefit: Coverdale, for example, admires her exceptional needlework when she fashions a nightcap for him during his convalescence.) Similarly, when Mercy first meets Christiana, the older woman cannot be sure what to do with her, but finally decides to take her: "I will hire thee, and thou shalt go along with me as my servant. Yet we will have all things in common betwixt thee and me; only, go along with me" (p. 177). Like Priscilla, Mercy is especially distinguished because of her skill with the needle: "When she had nothing to do for herself, she would be making of hose and garments for others, and would bestow them upon them that had need . . ." (p. 231). The careful obscurity with which Hawthorne clothes Priscilla's past, revealing it only as the story develops, has its counterpart in *The Pilgrim's Progress.* Mercy's past is obscure, and she speaks guardedly, not always giving her reasons for her actions. Only midway in the story do we learn the details of her past life, and here the parallels with Priscilla's past are more than coincidental: "Well, said Mercy, if nobody will have me I will die a maid, or my conditions shall be to me as a husband; for I cannot change my nature: and to have one that lies cross to me in this, that I purpose never to admit of as long as I live. I had a sister, named Bountiful, married to one of those churls: but he and she could never agree; but, because my sister was resolved to do as she had begun, that is, to show kindness to the poor, therefore her husband first cried her down at the cross,[25] and then turned her out of his doors" (p. 201). Priscilla's own bountiful sister is Zenobia, and Zenobia's past is darkened by the suggestion of her early unfortunate marriage, with a husband who disapproved of her "kindness to the poor."

If Bunyan's Mercy-Christiana relationship affords some parallels to Hawthorne's Priscilla-Zenobia sisterhood, then of even greater interest is the relationship between Priscilla and Hollingsworth. Eventually, of course, Hollingsworth is to be observed by Coverdale[26] as a miserable and broken-hearted man whose sole spiritual support seems to come from a now stronger Priscilla; but at the beginning of the romance the roles are reversed, and Priscilla turns to Hollingsworth for protection and comfort, much as a daughter might turn to her father. In this respect her actions are similar to those of Mercy when she asks the advice of Great-heart.

"Poor child!" exclaimed Zenobia, rather contemptuously. "She is the type of womanhood, such as man has spent centuries in making it. He is never content unless he can degrade himself by stooping towards what he loves. In denying us our rights, he betrays even more blindness to his own interests than profligate disregard of ours!"

"Is this true?" asked Priscilla, with simplicity, turning to Hollingsworth. "Is it all true, that Mr. Coverdale and Zenobia have been saying?"

"No, Priscilla!" answered Hollingsworth, with his customary bluntness. "They have neither of them spoken one true word yet."

"Do you despise woman [sic]?" said Zenobia. "Ah, Hollingsworth, that would be most ungrateful!"

"Despise her? No!" cried Hollingsworth, lifting his great shaggy head and shaking it at us, while his eyes glowed almost fiercely. "She is the most admirable handiwork of God, in her true place and character. Her place is at man's side. Her office, that of the sympathizer; the unreserved, unquestioning believer. . . ." [p. 511]

Great-heart's customary role in *The Pilgrim's Progress* is similar to Hollingsworth's in *The Blithedale Romance.* He is a guide, a protector of women (in their "true place and character"), a catechist, and a dogmatist. He disapproves heartily (just as Hollingsworth does in *Blithedale*) of those pilgrims who stray from the straight path.[27]

One of the most decisive parallels in the two works is seen in Hollingsworth's rescue of Priscilla from the worldly Professor Westervelt (whose identity with the devil is perhaps too obvious), and its original in Mercy's Dream in *The Pilgrim's Progress.* In the chapter entitled "The Village Hall," Priscilla, as the Veiled Lady, is being exhibited on the stage of the local Lyceum. Hollingsworth, searching for her, is in the audience. "The smell of corruption," so it seems to Coverdale, hangs over Westervelt's sham show. The Veiled Lady gropes towards her chair dreamily, like a "blindfolded prisoner." The eyes of all the spectators are upon her, and as Westervelt's spectacle approaches its climax, she rises unexpectedly:

The spectators, it may be, imagined that she was about to take flight into that invisible sphere, and to the society of those purely spiritual beings with whom they reckoned her so near akin. Hollingsworth, a moment ago, had mounted the platform, and now stood gazing at the figure, with a sad intentness that brought the whole power of his great, stern, yet tender soul into his glance. "Come," said he, waving his hand towards her. "You are safe!" She threw off the veil, and stood before that multitude of people, pale, tremulous, shrinking, as if only then had she discovered that a thousand eyes were gazing at her. Poor maiden! . . . She uttered a shriek, and fled to Hollingsworth, like one escaping from her deadliest enemy, and was safe forever. [p. 559]

Compare this scene from *Blithedale* with Mercy's account of her dream in *The Pilgrim's Progress:*

I was a dreaming that I sat all alone in a solitary place, and was bemoaning of the hardness of my heart. Now I had not sat there long, but methought many were gathered about me to see me, and to hear what it was that I said. So they hearkened, and I went on bemoaning the hardness of my heart. At this, some of them laughed at me, some called me fool, and some began to thrust me about [in *Blithedale,* some bumpkins had actually been invited upon the stage to toss the Veiled Lady into the air in an attempt to discompose her]. With that, methought I looked up, and saw one coming with wings towards me. So he came directly to me, and said, "Mercy, what aileth thee?" Now when he had heard me make my complaint, he said "Peace be to thee:" He also wiped mine eyes with his handkerchief, and clad me in silver and gold. He put a chain upon my neck, and earrings in mine ears, and a beautiful crown upon my head. Then he took me by the hand, and said, "Mercy, come after me." [p. 198]

As Hollingsworth rescues Priscilla, he also makes a choice against Zenobia, and even judges her. Thus in the very next chapter following Hollingsworth's rescue of Priscilla, we find Zenobia described as a dethroned queen. It is Priscilla who is "saved" by the great-hearted Hollingsworth, not Zenobia.

Very near the beginning of *The Blithedale Romance,* it is evident that Hawthorne may have intended his portrait of Hollingsworth to have been modeled after, and to depend for some of its strength upon, Great-heart, who was probably the most familiar of all imaginary spiritual guides to an audience of American readers in the middle of the nineteenth century. This intention is reflected in the scene where Zenobia, awaiting Hollingsworth's arrival, discusses his character with Coverdale: "Do you know Hollingsworth personally?" I inquired. "No; only as an . . . auditress . . . of some of his lectures," said she. "What a voice he has! and what a man he is! Yet not so much an intellectual man, I should say, as a great heart; at least, he moved me more deeply than I think myself capable of being moved . . ." (p. 451).

The Bunyan original for Hollingsworth had certain qualities which made him suitable for a guide. Great-heart was a servant of the Interpreter, and it was his duty to conduct pilgrims along the way from the Interpreter's House to the Land of Beulah. In the case of Christiana, Mercy, and the children, his instructions had originally been to guide them only as far as the Palace Beautiful; however, their need for him seemed to be so strong, that they prevailed upon him to ask his master if he could accompany them farther along the road. The weaker the pilgrim—physically, mentally, or spiritually (granted that he had the desire to be a pilgrim at all), the more would he be in need of the services and protection of Great-heart. Thus, in Part Two of *The Pilgrim's Progress,* it is appropriate for Great-heart to be called upon specifically to conduct a woman deserted by her husband, the woman's feeble maidservant, her children, and certain travellers picked up along the way such as Feeble-Mind and Honest. Great-heart is a battler, and he is at his best in his sword, helmet, and shield, when he is confronting antagonists who wish to impede the progress of the pilgrims in his care. Yet, because he is in the employ of the Interpreter, Great-heart is also a dialectician, and it is he who clarifies difficult points of doctrine for Christiana, Mercy, and the children. But most important: Great-heart himself is not a pilgrim! Perhaps the quality which most touches a reader of the Second Part of *The Pilgrim's Progress* is the open-heartedness and gentleness of this large-headed, shaggy man who guides so many pilgrims safely through the hazards of the road only to leave them at the "river which has no bridge." Here they receive instructions from the other side to cross over, while he who was responsible for their arrival at the river's edge must return to guide more pilgrims along the way. In the Valley of Humiliation (his favorite place) he says, "I have gone through this valley many a time. . . . I have also been a conductor to several Pilgrims." His view of life, although it is single-minded and narrow, is mature and thoughtful, and even philosophical. When he is in the Valley of the Shadow of Death, protecting Christiana and her family, he says,

> This is like doing business in great waters, or like going down into the deep; this is like being in the heart of the sea, and like going down to the bottoms of the mountains. . . . For my part, as I have told you already, I have gone often through this valley, and have been much harder put to it than now I am, and yet you see I am alive. I would not boast, for that I am not mine own Saviour; but I trust we shall have a good deliverance. Come, let us pray for light to him that can lighten our darkness, and that can rebuke not only these, but all the Satans in hell. [p. 209]

That Great-heart was at least in part the model for Hollingsworth becomes more clear when we notice the capacities of that "large, shaggy reformer." When Coverdale is, by his own admission, "in a state of moral as well as bodily faint-heartedness," Hollingsworth's effect upon him is similar to Great-heart's upon Mr. Fearing. What Great-heart says of Mr. Fearing applies equally to Coverdale in *Blithedale:*

> Every thing frighted him that he heard any body speak of, that had put the least appearance of opposition in it. I hear that he lay roaring at the Slough of Despond for above a month together; nor durst he, for all he saw several go over before him, venture, though they, many of them, offered to lend him their hand! He would not go back again neither.[28] The Celestial City! He said he should die if he came not to it; and yet he was dejected at every difficulty, and stumbled at every straw that any body cast in his way. [p. 213]

Great-heart's description of Mr. Fearing at the Palace Beautiful recalls the role Coverdale first played at Blithedale: "I got him in at the House Beautiful, I think, before he was willing; also, when he was in, I brought him acquainted with the damsels that were of the place, but he was ashamed to make himself much for company. He desired much to be alone, yet he always loved good talk, and often would get behind the screen to hear it. He also loved much to see ancient things, and to be pondering them in his mind" (p. 214). Coverdale's habit of leaving the community to wander in the near-by fields and woods recalls Great-heart's description of Mr. Fearing in the Valley of Humiliation: "I think there was a kind of sympathy betwixt that Valley and him; for I never saw him better in all his pilgrimage than when he was in that Valley. Here he would lie down, embrace the ground, and kiss the very flowers that grew in this valley" (p. 214). Coverdale actually becomes one with the landscape near Blithedale, as in his passionate eating of the grapes in his pine-tree arbor. Just as Mr. Fearing could not proceed upon his pilgrimage without the aid of Great-heart, so Coverdale confesses the need for Hollingsworth, the powerful healer:

There was something of the woman moulded into the great stalwart frame of Hollingsworth; nor was he ashamed of it, as men often are of what is best in them, nor seemed ever to know that there was such a soft place in his heart. I knew it well, however, at that time, although afterwards it came nigh to be forgotten. Methought there could not be two such men alive as Hollingsworth. There was never any blaze of a fireside that warmed and cheered me, in the downsinkings and shiverings of my spirit, so effectually as did the light out of those eyes, which lay so deep and dark under his shaggy brows.

Happy the man that has such a friend beside him when he comes to die. . . . It still impresses me as almost a matter of regret that I did not die then . . . for Hollingsworth would have gone with me to the hither verge of life, and have sent his friendly and hopeful accents far over on the other side, while I should be treading the unknown path. [p. 463]

Great-heart had conducted Mr. Fearing to "the hither verge of life," and then had taken his leave of him, wishing him "a good reception above."

In *The Blithedale Romance,* the principal characters, although modeled to some degree after the principal characters in the Second Part of *The Pilgrim's Progress,* represent a considerable distortion and alteration from the originals. Blithedale itself is similar on the interior to the House Beautiful; on the exterior, to the Enchanted Ground:[29] "You know [says Great-heart], when men talk in their sleep, they say any thing, but their words are not governed by either faith or reason. There is an incoherency in their words now. . . . This then is the mischief on't, when heedless ones go on pilgrimage, it is twenty to one but they are served thus. For this Enchanted Ground is one of the last refuges that the enemy to pilgrims has; wherefore it is, as you see, placed almost at the end of the way . . . nigh to the Land of Beulah" (p. 237).

Blithedale is the Enchanted Ground, and its participants are, at least in Hollingsworth's opinion, heedless ones who have gone on a pilgrimage. The sham quality of Blithedale is actually well known even to its principal participants. Coverdale withdraws and observes it from a convenient hideaway midway between the community and the city. Hollingsworth is simply invited to accompany these transcendental pilgrims in their pilgrimage, but he himself is described as a priest whose vocation is evidently to "spend [his] days and nights in helping [his] fellow-creatures to draw peaceful dying breaths" (p. 463). Hollingsworth, speaking of himself, says, "I should . . . say that the most marked trait in my character is an inflexibility of purpose. Mortal man has no right to be so inflexible as it is my nature and necessity to be" (p. 464). He is violently anti-Fourieristic (p. 470), and he acts like a "Puritan magistrate holding inquest of life and death in a case of witchcraft" (p. 565).

In the concluding chapters of *The Blithedale Romance*, Hollingsworth resembles a Great-heart distorted. Zenobia says to him that ". . . a great and rich heart has been ruined in your breast," and Coverdale says of him, "I see in Hollingsworth an exemplification of the most awful truth in Bunyan's book of such—from the very gate of heaven there is a by-way to the pit" (p. 583).[30] Hollingsworth conceives of himself as a heart-murderer. It is his probing which finally discovers Zenobia's body in the stream, and his thrust, ironically, had wounded her breast close to the heart. When Hollingsworth judged Zenobia, it was by nonhuman standards: "I have judged you, but not on the world's part,—neither do I pretend to pass a sentence" (p. 565). Like Bunyan's Great-heart, he views himself as a conductor of pilgrims to the gates of the Celestial City, but he remembers his duty always to return, and never to enter the gates himself. Ironically, he is at last guided by a girl—forced to lean upon Priscilla (Mercy) for support.

The clue to Hollingsworth's character is also the clue to the character of the original Great-heart, for Great-heart is not Bunyan's allegorical Christian, and he is not himself on a pilgrimage. Thus, when the pilgrims, under his guidance, arrive at the Land of Beulah, he must himself return to his master, the Interpreter. Perhaps this is the reason why he is so taken with the Valley of Humiliation, and why Hollingsworth is so attracted by the quiet landscapes around Blithedale. Of the Valley of Humiliation, Great-heart says,

> It is the best and most fruitful piece of ground in all these parts. It is fat ground, and, as you see, consisteth much in meadows; and if a man was to come here in the summer-time, as we do now, if he knew not anything before thereof, and if he also delighted himself in the sight of his eyes, he might see that which would be delightful to him. Behold, how green this Valley is, also how beautiful with lilies. I have also known many labouring men that have got good estates in the Valley . . . , for indeed it is a very fruitful soil, and doth bring forth by handfuls. Some also have wished, that the next way to their Father's house were here, that they might be troubled no more with either hills or mountains to go over; but the way is the way, and there is an end. [p. 206]

Hollingsworth's feelings about the Blithedale countryside are similar to these, but he himself admits that inflexibility of purpose is the principal part of his character—the way is the way, and there is an end. No matter how many times he went to the "certain point on the slope of a pasture," with its commanding view of Blithedale, the river, and distant hills, ultimately he could not be content at Blithedale.

I have suggested that the Second Part of *The Pilgrim's Progress* influenced Hawthorne's creation of characters and character-relationships in *The Blithedale Romance.* Bunyan's Second Part differs in many ways from his First, and is generally considered to be inferior. Whereas the central character of the First Part is a solitary man intent upon saving his soul at all cost, the Second Part describes the somewhat less arduous journey of some women and children in search of a husband, a father, and salvation. The journey of these women and children is made less arduous not only because the many pitfalls which betrayed Christian have been cleaned up, eliminated, or repaired, but also because the women are accompanied by the remarkable character Great-heart—a strong, fatherly, doctrinal man, not a pilgrim himself, who most enjoys antagonism.

The Blithedale Romance depends in some degree, then, upon just such relationships. Blithedale itself is a curiously feminine community. Its communicants consider themselves pilgrims who intend to bring about the salvation of the world and to establish the New Jerusalem, and consequently the writings of Emerson and the articles in *The Dial* are "well-adapted . . . to pilgrims like [them]-selves, whose present bivouac was considerably further into the waste of chaos than any mortal army of crusaders had ever marched before" (p. 469). Zenobia and her secret-sister Priscilla call to mind Christiana and Mercy in Bunyan's allegory. Hawthorne's Priscilla and Bunyan's Mercy are faint maidservants and skillful seamstresses who attach themselves in an uncomfortable proximity to their strong-willed and older female companions, but allow themselves at the same time to be guided and protected by a powerful, fatherly, great-hearted man. Coverdale is a Mr. Fearing who is neither a part of, nor entirely separate from, the rest of the community: he wants to go to the Celestial City, but, as Great-heart said of the original Mr. Fearing, "he had, I think, a Slough of Despond in his mind, a slough that he carried every where with him , or else he could never have been as he was" (p. 213). Hollingsworth is, as Zenobia says early in the novel, a "great heart" (p. 451).

There are other less direct influences of Bunyan in *The Blithedale Romance*—the reflected image of the House Beautiful and the Enchanted Ground in the Blithedale community; the reflection of Vanity Fair in Coverdale's description of Boston-town; and, as in all of Hawthorne's fiction, the heavy reliance upon the imagery of pathways. But the most important influences upon Hawthorne's imagination seem to me to be those I have suggested above.

If the First Part of *The Pilgrim's Progress* is imaginatively reflected in *The Scarlet Letter*, then it is the Second Part which is imaginatively useful in *The Blithedale Romance*. The importance of Hawthorne's almost intuitive use of Bunyanesque imagery, allegory, and characterization lies not only in its indication of his deep and often-acknowledged indebtedness to Bunyan, nor even only in the implication that he was writing for a generation which was Bunyan-saturated in a way that our generation is not—but rather in the fact that yet a broader and deeper meaning may be supported by his art if we make ourselves aware of the depth, the richness, and the complexity of its sources. *The Pilgrim's Progress* impressed its enormous weight upon the writing of Nathaniel Hawthorne more than did any other single work. In "The Celestial Railroad," he chose to acknowledge his indebtedness to Bunyan directly by writing an up-to-date version of *The Pilgrim's Progress*. But it would be a mistake to conclude that the influence of Bunyan's work could find reflection only overtly in Hawthorne's art. *The Pilgrim's Progress* was deeply imbedded in his creative consciousness, and we are likely to find unexpected and often luxuriant blossomings from it throughout the range of his imaginative production. It has been the purpose of this chapter to suggest where a few of these hidden flowers may be found.

IV

LITTLE WOMEN: A POSTWAR *PILGRIM'S PROGRESS*

For little tripping maids may follow God
Along the ways which saintly feet have trod.

"Behold, ye, how these crystal streams do glide,
To comfort-pilgrims by the high-way side,
The meadows green besides their fragrant smell,
Yield dainties for them ; and he that can tell
What pleasing fruit, yea, leaves, these trees do yield,
Will soon sell all, that he may buy this field."

THE PILGRIM'S PROGRESS

New York, Harper, 1837

Frontispiece engraved by Joseph Alexander Adams after design by John G. Chapman. Even as the allegory was being romanticized or domesticated by authors such as Lousia May Alcott, so also were the pictorial representations of Christian's journey.

Chapter Four

A VIVID demonstration of the shift which took place in American attitudes towards Bunyan following the Civil War may be found in the purposes which *The Pilgrim's Progress* is made to serve in *Little Women.*[1] Significantly, two of the most successful writers of juvenile books in the second half of the nineteenth century—Miss Alcott and Samuel Clemens—were the only important authors to use *The Pilgrim's Progress* (influential "juvenile" of their own youth) overtly in their published works.[2]

The war seemed to mark a division between a time when, for most Americans, *The Pilgrim's Progress* was invested with the sanctity of an oracle, and a later time when its intention was misunderstood, its meaning reversed, and its seriousness ridiculed. The generation which subjected *The Pilgrim's Progress* to such treatment may be said to have been the last generation in America which had read the great allegory seriously as a childhood experience, and if the book was still an oracle to their aging fathers, the children, no matter how seriously impressed they were by Christian's journey, found themselves growing up in a world of changing values and new experiences in which the original nature of the pilgrimage seemed less directly relevant to their lives. If Christian's journey was to have meaning for them, it would only be after they had transformed it so that it would somehow assume pertinence to their contemporary world. Their fathers had justified Bunyan because his work, in turn, could be employed to justify the excesses of a desperate latter-day Calvinism,[3] but for children born in the 1830's, like Miss Alcott and Clemens, who would normally have read *The Pilgrim's Progress* in the 1840's during the last period of its prolific publication in America, Bunyan's enduring allegory assumed new, and usually paler, meanings.

Inasmuch as the Civil War had its effect upon this generation of readers and writers, it destroyed, in great degree, the image of *The Pilgrim's Progress* as a meaningful one in the American mind, although the book remained familiar enough in the seventies and eighties so that it could be confidently referred to. Two anecdotes, both originating in the 1880's, illustrate this fact. Moncure Conway,[4] watching a dramatic production of *The Pilgrim's Progress,* overheard "a devout church lady" whispering "Are we expected to admire [Christian] for running away and leaving his family in the City of Destruction?"[5] An incident of similar import occurs in *Huckleberry Finn* when Huck describes a copy of *The Pilgrim's Progress* at the Grangerfords: "One [book] was *Pilgrim's Progress,* about a man that left his family, it didn't say why. I read considerable in it now and then. The statements was interesting, but tough."[6] What these two amusing anecdotes suggest is a radical shift of focus. Conway confessed that his own mind had changed since he followed "Bunyan's Pilgrim with heart palpitant with enthusiasm," and that the change in himself in thirty years "was as complete as if [he] had been born into another race."[7]

It is no accident that in her most successful book Miss Alcott should find Bunyan's work useful, because her own childhood had been strongly influenced by his almost continual presence. In the Alcott family, it was the father who stimulated the children not only to read *The Pilgrim's Progress* but to play at it so hard that ultimately the characters would become as much a reality to them as they had become to Alcott. Alcott's first reading of *The Pilgrim's Progress* "was a religious experience, in some ways amounting to a 'conversion,' "[8] and subsequently he was to model his own life on Christian's in the sense that it would be a pilgrimage "from this world to that which is to come." Alcott's mature recollections of the importance which the book held for him as a youth suggest that the realities of the imaginary world of the allegory became more vivid to him than reality itself.[9] Moncure Conway recorded a similar experience, remembering that "Apollyon and other foes" did not yet belong to Fairy land in his childhood,[10] but were physical realities. Such a notion becomes important when we consider *Little Women,* for here the essential theme of the story is that the four girls, who *played* at Bunyan when they were much younger, must now make him an actuality, must "live" *The Pilgrim's Progress:* "Mrs. March . . . [said] in her cheery voice, 'Do you remember how you used to play Pilgrim's Progress when you were little things? Nothing delighted you more then than to have me tie my piece-bags on your backs for burdens, give you hats and sticks, and rolls of paper, and let you travel through the house from the cellar, which was the City of Destruction, up, up, to the house-top, where you had all the lovely things you could collect to make a Celestial City.' "[11] The children recall with delight the fun they had, and Amy thinks they should play the game again, even though they are all now teen-agers. Mrs. March agrees: "We are never too old for this, my dear, because it is a play we are playing all the time in one way or another. Our burdens are here, our road is before us, and the longing for goodness and happiness is the guide that leads us through many troubles and mistakes to the peace which is a true Celestial City. Now my little pilgrims, suppose you begin again, not in play, but in earnest, and see how far you can get before father comes home."[12] Thus, for the March girls, the play world becomes the real world, and life itself in its most serious aspects is best approached as if it were a game. The game chosen as a proper guide of life itself is the Game of Pilgrim's Progress.[13] It is clear that Bunyan had come to be seen in a different light by a family, or a society, which could make *Pilgrim's Progress* into a game, but it should also be clear that the level of seriousness of the idea of games is raised considerably when the object of the game is a spiritual pilgrimage, and when the players are made aware that the stakes are, in effect, real ones.

Louisa May Alcott grew up in a family which believed that play was a serious approach to life, and Bronson Alcott's "revolutionary" theories of education embraced the idea that the best way to learn something was by playing at it, by making a game of it.[14] *Little Women,* as a result, may be regarded as a document full of contradictions and paradoxes—a game is life itself; children are adults; women are men; home is the world—and it is probably these paradoxes which have contributed to its perennial popularity: juvenile readers can take the book seriously, because it is a book which at all times takes itself seriously.[15] It is intended to be as much a guide to correct social behavior as *The Pilgrim's Progress* was believed to be a guide to proper spiritual behavior a generation earlier. If we are to approach *Little Women* as something more than an immensely popular book for girls, and if we are to regard it as an index of popular taste in manners and morals in the second half of the nineteenth century, then we must to some degree be bound by the book's own assertions, that is, that life is a serious game to be played according to certain rules. As it happens, the rule book is *Pilgrim's Progress,* but an analysis of the way the game is played (and thus how life is lived by a middle-class, postwar American family) will reveal that the greatest reversal of all occurs in the image of the pilgrims and the nature of the pilgrimage.

Three things unify *Little Women.* The first, and perhaps the most superficial, is the device of the months of the year. The story is developed chronologically according to the seasons, beginning at one Christmastime, with Father absent, and concluding with the next Christmas, when Father has just returned, an invalid from the war. The second unifying force in the book is the controlling image of the home, with Mother at its center. Almost everything important which happens to the March family happens within the confines of the home, and if anything happens outside the home, it is, as a rule, reported in the home rather than directly described. The Civil War, for example, exists for the Marches because Father is absent at it. When he falls seriously ill, and Mrs. March leaves to help him in Washington, we see only her departure, and are informed of her activities during her absence by letters which arrive "back home."

This centripetal focus, achieved through the development of the physical image of the house itself, becomes important as we consider the third unifying force in the book, which is the Game of Pilgrim's Progress. Mrs. March, as we have seen, persuades her four daughters that, during the year of their father's absence from home, they should become pilgrims. Each should assume a burden, and each should consider herself on a pilgrimage in the direction of the Celestial City. Assumption of a burden becomes, for each girl, the identification and recognition of her principal moral weakness (paradoxically also the source of each girl's charm): Jo's burden is her sharp tongue and quick temper; Meg's is her interest in worldly things, including her own physical beauty, and so on. The pilgrimage, for Bunyan one in space, becomes in *Little Women* one in time (the period of one war-year).

The device of the Game of Pilgrim's Progress is central to the meaning of *Little Women,* and it would undoubtedly have been the assumption of Miss Alcott that all of her little (and big) readers were familiar with Bunyan's *Pilgrim's Progress.* Later generations of readers, less and less likely to have read Bunyan, may well have received their first and only introduction to him through the pages of *Little Women,* and if this is true, their view of *The Pilgrim's Progress* would be distorted. We may see this most dramatically, perhaps, if we compare Bunyan's pilgrim and his pilgrimage with the March pilgrims and theirs. In the first place, Bunyan's Christian leaves home and family, and it is necessary for him to do so. Miss Alcott's pilgrims remain at home, while the father, like Christian, has deserted the family to fight a Holy War.[16] But whereas Christian was healthy and vital and adequately prepared for his pilgrimage, which the reader is invited to follow, Mr. March is unhealthy, unprepared for the rigors of the war, and totally outside the framework of the story. When we are finally introduced to the poor man, he is represented as a helpless invalid surrounded by lively and competent nurses.[17] Bunyan's Christian pursues the greater part of his pilgrimage after his burden has dropped from his back, but for Miss Alcott's pilgrims, the burden to be carried defines the act of pilgrimage. The most significant difference between the two pilgrimages, however, is that whereas Christian leaves home to journey through a wilderness towards the Celestial City, the March girls view their own home as the world, and literally conduct their pilgrimage within it. As children they had found it fanciful to consider the cellar as the City of Destruction and the garret as the Celestial City, but when we consider the degree to which house and home embody thematic meaning in *Little Women,* it becomes dramatically evident that in the "real" playing of the game, things have not changed. Home is the Celestial City, and home is also where the pilgrimage must be made. When the girls have met one summer's day upon a hilltop, all dressed to resemble Christian, they are surprised by Laurie, the boy next door. When he promises to keep a secret, he is initiated into the secret "society," and the girls explain to him the inner meaning of their actions: "Well, you see, we used to play 'Pilgrim's Progress,' and we have been going on with it in earnest, all winter and summer."[18] The girls inform Laurie that the hill they are on is the Delectable Mountain, where they can "look far away and see the country where we hope to live sometime" (p. 206). After discussing their feelings about election into the Celestial City, the children describe their own notions about it, and, with the single exception of Amy, the youngest and least "mature," the girls see Heaven as home. Meg wants "a lovely house, full of all sorts of luxurious things,—nice food, pretty clothes, handsome furniture, pleasant people, and heaps of money" (p. 208). Beth, the frail sister, dreams of staying "at home safe with father and mother" (p. 209), and Jo's house would have "rooms piled with books" (p. 209).

But it is not merely in their dreams of the Celestial City that the little pilgrims associate it with the typical middle-class home. The garret of the March house is also (as it had been in the early childhood game) a Celestial City

cessful pilgrimage—the one which resulted not in banishment from Eden but in transforming home itself into Paradise—is represented imaginatively in *Little Women.*

The paradox of *Little Women* is that, although Vanity Fair is represented superficially by the elegance, conspicuous consumption, and vicarious leisure of the Moffats, whom Meg visits on a holiday, ultimately the dreams of such elegance control the hopes and destinies of the Little Women themselves. Vanity Fair dominates *Little Women,* in spite of Miss Alcott's intentions to the contrary, and ultimately each girl (with the exception of Beth, who dies) becomes rich, not poor; fashionable, not unfashionable; and happy, not miserable. To put it another way, Bunyan's Christian, were he to have returned to Concord in 1870, would have regarded the circumstances of all the March girls as smacking of the Cities of Destruction and Carnality. The kind of pilgrimage undertaken by the March girls (and thereby recommended to all young readers of Miss Alcott's didactic books) led ultimately only as far as the City of Vanity, although readers in the second half of the nineteenth century would more likely call it "heavenly home." Why, they would ask, should anyone ever wish to leave it?

It was inevitable that a society for whom the medieval Christian concept of a spiritual quest had lost all meaning would translate it into the banal and mediocre language of middle-class sentimental piety.

V

THE ENORMOUS ROOM, *THE PILGRIM'S PROGRESS,* AND THE "DEMONIC TRINITY"

Behold Vanity-Fair! the pilgrims there
Are chain'd and stow'd beside:
Even so it was, Our Lord pass'd here,
And on Mount Calvary dy'd.

THE PILGRIM'S PROGRESS
Philadelphia, M'Culloch, 1793

Chapter Five

IT IS QUITE POSSIBLE THAT E. E. Cummings chose *The Pilgrim's Progress* as the organizing principle of *The Enormous Room*[1] because he well knew that for most people in his generation its spiritual power and moral lessons were either forgotten or misunderstood. *The Enormous Room* is, therefore, an intentional *Pilgrim's Progress.* The striking difference is that in a world made nauseous, in Hemingway's phrase, "as the result of untruth or exaggeration," where "all our words from loose using have lost their edge," Cummings chose a radical method to reinstate the truths of *The Pilgrim's Progress.* He was not immediately understood.

The Enormous Room shocked not only the complacent and the prudish in its generation of readers, but even contemporary reviewers who were otherwise ready to admire the youthful Cummings' verbal experiments. P. L. Masson, in the *New York Times,*[2] admitted with considerable reserve that "apart from its crudities . . . the book [was] quite worthwhile"; the *Detroit News* reviewer, D. K. Lamb, felt that "the author could have succeeded . . . without being so gratuitously filthy";[3] and the reviewer for the *Boston Transcript*[4] contrasted the book's "exquisite finesse in portraiture" with its "brutal inchoate raving [dissolving] into a maze of meaningless word sounds." Two reviewers—John Dos Passos in *Dial* (July, 1922) and

Ben Ray Redman in the *Nation* (June 7, 1922)—praised the new book unequivocally. Dos Passos, a fellow-student in what Alfred Kazin has called "the finishing school of the lost generation: the Norton-Harjes ambulance corps,"[5] compared *The Enormous Room* to Defoe's *Journal of the Plague Year,* and Redman protected the author's prose style from the attacks of "certain nice-stomached gentry" who had "manifested nausea at Mr. Cummings' use of language." Redman, more than any other contemporary reviewer, seems to have understood a deeper intention in *The Enormous Room* when he described Cummings' "weapon" as that of "one who has experienced an overwhelming pity not for his fellow-prisoners but for the outside world that made the room possible."

What Masson in the *Times* review had missed was everything. It was not apart from its crudities that the book was "quite worthwhile," but because of them. Cummings deliberately wrote a shocking book, but his ultimate intention was not merely to shock: it was to construct, symbolically, a Paradise within an Inferno—a Celestial City upon the ruins of the City of Destruction. If Christian could no longer journey to the Delectable Mountains, Cummings would bring the Delectable Mountains to Christian.

ii

For half its length, the narrator's journey resembles Christian's in *The Pilgrim's Progress.*[6] Only the obtuse would require the careful résumé at midpoint in the narrative: "In the preceding pages I have described my Pilgrim's Progress from the Slough of Despond, commonly known as *Section Sanitaire Vingt-et-un* (then located at Germaine) through the mysteries of Noyon, Gré and Paris to the Porte de Triage de La Ferté Macé, Orne" (p. 130). The parallel journey is spiritual, not literal, yet the identification of the narrator with Christian is illuminated at crucial instances in such a way as to reflect a fundamental dependence upon the earlier allegory. The prisoner's burden, consisting of a huge duffel bag and a bed roll, represents for him the same weight of sin, the same cumbersome conscience of the guilty man, as it did for Christian. When he is able to put the burden down, he is "himself" (p. 45). When he checks his burden at the end of the eventful train-ride to Briouse, he has arrived psychologically at the identical point at which Christian was relieved of his burden—he is at the Cross:

> Uphill now. Every muscle thoroughly aching, head spinning, I half-straightened my no longer obedient body; and jumped: face to face with a little wooden man hanging all by itself in a grove of low trees.
>
> The wooden body clumsy with pain burst into fragile legs with absurdly large feet and funny writhing toes. . . . About its stunted loins clung a ponderous and jocular fragment of drapery. On one terribly brittle shoulder the droll lump of its neckless head ridiculously lived. . . .
>
> For perhaps a minute the almost obliterated face and mine eyed one another in the silence of intolerable autumn.
>
> Who was this wooden man? Like a sharp, black, mechanical cry in the spongy organism of gloom stood the coarse and sudden sculpture of his torment; the big mouth of night carefully spurted the angular actual language of his martyred body. I had seen him before in the dream of some mediaeval saint with a thief sagging at either side, surrounded with crisp angels. Tonight he was alone; save for myself, and the moon's minute flower pushing between slabs of fractured cloud. [p. 75]

Now the narrator is one of the Elect; and only from this crucial point may his spiritual progress be measured. Having lost his burden at the Cross, Cummings enters into that terrifying Interpreter's House, the Enormous Room, which is to be transformed through human courage until it permits a view of the Delectable Mountains.

Like all initiates into the mysteries, the narrator has become *Le Nouveau*. "With the end of my first day as a certified inhabitant of [La Ferté Macé] a definite progression is brought to a close. Beginning with my second day at La Ferté a new period opens. [It] extends to the moment of my departure and includes the discovery of the Delectable Mountains . . ." (p. 130).

Cummings' rebirth into the Society of the Enormous Room shares superficially in the conventional religious symbolism of conversion: he is baptized (in a chilling *douche*); he partakes of a kind of communion; the room gradually fills with light; *Le Nouveau* is not immediately aware of the full significance of the mysteries. The pilgrim is confronted by an Infernal Trinity[7] symbolizing the world, the flesh, and the devil. However, the existence of this traditional Infernal Trinity in *The Enormous Room* is overshadowed by the hovering presence of a far subtler Trinity, one which has been ingeniously suggested (in other contexts) by Professor Kenneth Burke: "The substantial nature of imagery may often produce an unintended burlesque of substance, in drawing upon the ambiguities of the cloacal, where there are united, in a 'demonic trinity,' the three principles of the erotic, urinary, and excremental. . . . Images from the cloacal sources are basic to the 'thinking of the body'; and we may expect their privy nature to complicate the capitalist rationale of private property."[8] Whereas for Professor Burke the "demonic trinity" often finds expression in the " 'excremental' nature of invective or vilification" (e.g., a writer heaping "verbal offal" upon his opponent), *The Enormous*

Room manipulates the images of the erotic, urinary, and excremental to symbolize the most precious mysteries of Christian brotherhood. In not perceiving Cummings' extraordinary use of the "excremental," earlier critics of *The Enormous Room* have misunderstood the author's intention.[9]

Cleanliness is next to ungodliness in Cummings' ludicrously inverted scheme of things. The only physically clean beings are the nonprisoners. The "very definite fiend," Apollyon, who is the director of the prison, is an impeccable dresser, a terrifying little monster whose most disgusting feature is his inhuman fetish for personal cleanliness. We see him "shaking a huge fist of pinkish, well-manicured flesh, the distinct, cruel, brightish eyes sprouting from their sockets," as he adjusts his cuffs and mutters horrible insults to the women prisoners: "PROSTITUTES and WHORES and DIRTY FILTH OF WOMEN" (p. 174). It is a perfectly obvious irony that, behind his puppet-like facade of cleanliness, Apollyon is responsible for the filthiest of prisons.

Under such circumstances, human brotherhood remains possible only among the condemned. However, entrance into the Enormous Room is not by itself an initiation into the monastic community of the faithful, for there are some prisoners who resist conversion. A notable example is Count Bragard, the impostor.[10]

When Cummings first meets Bragard, he is not yet aware that the man is a hypocrite. Bragard is "immaculately apparelled in a crisp albeit collarless shirt, carefully mended trousers in which the remains of a crease still lingered, a threadbare but perfectly fitting swallow-tail coat, and newly varnished . . . shoes" (p. 92). The "Count," who poses as a painter, claims friendship with Cézanne. He is disgusted with his fellow-prisoners, whom he regards as swine: " 'This filth'—he pronounced the word with indescribable bitterness—'this herding of men like cattle—they treat us no better than pigs here. The fellows drop their dung in the very room where they sleep. What is one to expect of a place like this? *Ce n'est pas une existence*'—his French was glib and faultless" (p. 92). It is immediately after his introduction to Bragard that *Le Nouveau* undergoes the "cleansing" experience of the icy, dirty bath—a kind of baptism into the filth of the "unmistakably ecclesiastical" Enormous Room.

The theme is at once revolting and transcendent: human excrement, normally the object of universal disgust, symbolizes human brotherhood and, eventually, Christian salvation. The most prominent feature of the Enormous Room is its odor: "As you stood with your back to the door, and faced down the room, you had in the near right-hand corner . . . six pails of urine. On the right-hand long wall . . . a few boards tacked together . . . marked the position of a *cabinet d'aisance,* composed of a small coverless tin pail identical with the other six" (p. 90).

Le Nouveau painfully acquaints himself with those prisoner-friends who will become for him "Delectable Mountains"; even as he does so, he must reject the usual premium placed superficially upon general cleanliness. Finding himself in a comic, repugnant world which appears inexpressibly chaotic,[11] he must eventually arrive at the position of his friend "B" (a kind of Interpreter), who says, "Cummings, I tell you this is the finest place on earth!" (p. 85). *Le Nouveau's* friendships and loyalties develop to the degree that he is able to become one with the gaping, belching, trumpeting fraternity: he must be "swallowed by the Enormous Room." He must learn to consume, in company with his fellows, the "faintly-smoking urine-colored circular broth" (p. 113), and he must learn to trust this kind of communion while he rejects the hypocritical and even comical performance of the Holy Eucharist supervised by Apollyon:

> A *planton* mounted to the Enormous Room and shouted
>
> "La Messe!"
>
> several times; whereat the devotees lined up and were carefully conducted to the scene of spiritual operations.
>
> The priest was changed every week. His assistant . . . was always the same. It was his function to pick the priest up when he fell down after tripping upon his robe, to hand him things before he wanted them. . . . At moments of leisure he abased his fatty whitish jowl and contemplated with watery eyes the floor in front of his highly polished boots, having first placed his ugly chubby hands together behind his most ample back. [p. 187]

The conventional Mass reaches its ironical climax for the prisoners on a Sunday when a particularly thoughtless priest exhorts the forcibly assembled group—" '*Vous êtes libres, mes enfants, de faire l'immortalité. . . . Le ciel est fait pour vous*' . . . , and [Cummings observes] the Belgian ten-foot farmer spat three times and wiped them with his foot, his nose dripping; and the nigger shot a white oyster into a far-off scarlet handkerchief—and the Man's strings came untied and he sidled crab-like down the steps . . . " (p. 188).

Cummings' violent dismissal of the ordinary forms of things does not imply that he has rejected the ultimate spiritual meanings which the forms should symbolize. Civilization itself is unspeakably corrupt; it is reflected in the injustices of governments, the ironies of power struggles between nations, and the horrors of a chaotic and

meaningless war. In the microcosm of the Enormous Room it is represented by *Le Directeur,* by the Black Holster (brutal chief of the *plantons*), and by the "Three Wise Men" and their Inquisition. Above all, civilization's least satisfactory product is the unthinking and insensitive American, the incommunicative, middle-class, self-satisfied average man, represented here as "Mr. A.": "You boys want to keep away from those dirty Frenchmen. . . . We're here to show those bastards how they do things in America" (p. 27). Cummings' "war-time Mr. A."—section-chief of an ambulance service subsidized with Morgan money—reappears in the postwar poems in civilian clothes as the prototypical unthinking American. He is immortalized, in all of his anal fastidiousness, in the cynically portrayed subject of "Poem, or Beauty Hurts Mr. Vinal," defecating (with a hun-dred-mil-lion-oth-ers) on a "sternly allotted sandpile," emitting a "tiny violet-flavored nuisance: Odor?
ono."

What most disturbed Cummings in the immediate postwar years was a mass insensitivity to the distressing and, relevantly, stinking conditions of war (and, by extension, of civilization). Those who refused to use their noses except to avoid the actual smell of life became, like the Cambridge ladies of the sonnet, possessed of furnished souls and uncomfortable minds merely; their daughters, like their lives, were "unscented and shapeless."[12] *The Enormous Room* was addressed to this unscented majority in the hope that it would be not merely shocked but that it would sense, somehow, beyond its Wrigley's Spearmint, Nujolneeding, Odorono values, that Christian brotherhood existed among human odors, not beyond them. The new Samaritan of the poem "a man who had fallen among thieves," ignores the "frozen brook of pinkest vomit" to save his victim:

> Brushing from whom the stiffened puke
> i put him all into my arms
> and staggered banged with terror through
> a million billion trillion stars [.]

In choosing for his prototype fool the overcivilized American with a supersensitive nose, Cummings discovered an essential symbol. Inevitably, therefore, his own pilgrim would need to be able to smell his fellow human beings in order to progress with them toward the Delectable Mountains. In contrast, the impostor Count Bragard, who cannot tolerate the stink of his fellow-prisoners, is clearly identifiable with the worst excesses of modern civilization: he prostitutes his art; his real God is not Cézanne, but Vanderbilt.[13]

A genuine communion of the brotherhood of prisoners is suggested by the imposed necessity of their acting together rather than as individuals. During a journey of several nights and days, four prisoners were handcuffed wrist to wrist, and "the handcuffs were not once removed. The prisoners slept sitting up or falling over one another. They urinated and defecated with the handcuffs on, all of them hitched together" (p. 247). In a ludicrous scene, Apollyon surprises some women prisoners as they are "carrying their slops along the hall and down-stairs, as (in common with the men) they had to do at least twice every morning and twice every afternoon." Cummings describes "five or six women staggering and carrying pails full to the brim of everyone knew what; five or six heads, lowered, ill-dressed bodies tense with effort, free arms rigidly extended from the shoulder downward and outward in a plane at right angles to their difficult progress, and thereby helping to balance the disconcerting load—all embarrassed, some humiliated, others desperately at ease . . ." (p. 172). The sudden appearance of *Le Directeur* has its result: "I saw once a little girl of eleven years old scream in terror and drop her pail of slops, spilling most of it on her feet; and seize it in a clutch of frail child's fingers, and stagger, sobbing and shaking, past the Fiend—one hand held over her contorted face to shield her from the Awful Thing of Things—to the head of the stairs; where she collapsed, and was half-carried, half-dragged by the older ones to the floor below, while another older one picked up her pail and lugged this and her own hurriedly downward" (p. 173). On this occasion *Le Nouveau* declared that, for the only time in his life, he wanted to kill (p. 174).

iii

"In the course of the next ten thousand years," wrote Cummings after his return to New York, "it may be possible to find Delectable Mountains without going to prison" (p. 309). While he was in captivity, however, he found that communication was only possible with those "common scum" who had not been hopelessly indoctrinated by civilization. Bunyan's Worldly Wise-men, for Cummings, constituted the majority of the "monster manunkind." "The Great American Public," he wrote, had "a handicap which my friends at La Ferté did not as a rule have—education. Let no one sound his indignant yawp at this" (p. 309). Communication, then, in the Enormous Room, if it were to exist among the prisoners at all, had to be established upon some deeper principle than spoken language. The principle was that of a communion of the Elect. Words were inadequate: "Things . . . which are always inside of us and in fact are us and which consequently will not be pushed off or away where we can begin thinking about them—are no longer things; they, and the us which they are, equals A Verb; an IS. The Zulu, [one of Cummings' intimates, a "Delectable Mountain"] then, I must perforce call an IS" (p. 239). In speaking of this second of the four "Delectable Mountains," Cummings is careful to make the point that The Zulu spoke no conventionally communicable language, and yet "I have never in my life so perfectly understood (even to the most exquisite nuances) whatever idea another human being desired at any moment to communicate to me, as I have in the case of The Zulu" (p. 246). The secret of The Zulu's means of communication ". . . lay in that very essence which I have only defined as an IS; ended and began with an innate and unlearnable control over all which one can only describe as the homogeneously tactile" (p. 246).

The Delectable Mountains are those persons who embody, for the pilgrim, all possible human values—notwithstanding a totally corrupt civilization which has unjustly attempted to destroy them. They are, like The Zulu, incapable of ordinary discourse, but like him, communicate upon a deeper and more intuitive level. The "third Delectable Mountain," for example, was Surplice. No one was certain about his nationality. His words were "trying hard to be and never [could] be Polish" (p. 262). Surplice was a fool. He was "utterly ignorant," "utterly curious," "utterly hungry." His name was so badly mispronounced that the Belgians and Hollanders referred to him as "Syph'lis."[14] Surplice is intended as a symbol for Christ: the imagery of the chapter devoted to him is developed in a series of allusions to the Son of God."Of nobody can he say My Friend, of no one has he ever said or will he ever say My Enemy" (p. 262). Surplice's departure was like our Lord's: "We did our best to cheer him; we gave him a sort of Last Supper at our bedside, we heated some red wine in the tin-cup and he drank with us. . . . We offered him a cup of wine. A kind of huge convulsion gripped, for an instant, fiercely his entire face: then he said in a whisper of sheer and unspeakable wonderment . . . : '*Pour moi, monsieur*?' " (p. 272). Surplice, or Christ, is more clearly and repeatedly identified with human excrement than is any other character. Some of the prisoners despise him for it. "Every morning he takes the pail of solid excrement down, without anyone's suggesting that he take it; . . . he has, in fact, an obstreperous affinity for excrement; he lives in it" (p. 262). Surely, Cummings' deepest intention here is not merely to revolt the reader. This same Surplice, or Syph'-lis, is "intensely religious, religious with a terrible and exceedingly beautiful and absurd intensity" (p. 262). Clearly, the only revolted persons are the superficially fastidious who are also, in this setting, the inhuman. "Mr. A," the section-leader of the ambulance corps, had warned: "We gotta show we're superior to 'em. Those bastards doughno what a bath means. . . . If you want [privileges] you gotta shave and look neat, and *keep away from them dirty Frenchmen.* [Author's italics] We Americans are over here to learn them lousy bastards something" (p. 86). Implicit in "Mr. A's" attitude is the sniffy contempt which will characterize the provincial America of Cummings' postwar poems: we have deodorized ourselves out of existence.

The narrative of *The Enormous Room* concludes with *Le Nouveau's* departure from La Ferté Macé. (Actually, Cummings had been released from the French prison-camp largely through the deliberate efforts of his father, a Unitarian minister.) The emphasis, as in any rite of passage, is upon what the initiate has learned from his journey. In this instance, the maimed hero can never again regard the outer world (i.e. "civilization") without irony. But the spiritual lesson he learned from his sojourn with a community of brothers will be repeated in his subsequent writings both as an ironical dismissal of the values of his contemporary world, and as a sensitive, almost mystical celebration of the quality of Christian love.

iv

Even if we admit the ingenuity of Cummings' device in *The Enormous Room*, we may still ask whether the enormity of the conceit, developed so fully as it is, succeeds. Until one returns directly to Bunyan's allegory, he may forget just how scummy the Slough of Despond actually was. Bunyan implies that a virtually inescapable condition of man's spiritual salvation is that he "wallow for a time," and become "grievously bedaubed" (p. 92). Christian cannot help wondering why the place is not "mended, that poor Travellers might go . . . with more security," and his companion of the moment, Help, explains: "It is the descent whither the scum and filth that attends conviction for sin doth continually run, and therefore it is called the *Slough of Dispond*: for still as the sinner is awakened about his lost condition, there ariseth in his soul many fears, and doubts, and discouraging apprehensions, which all of them get together, and settle in this place; And this is the reason of the badness of this ground" (p. 92). Help clearly implies that the Slough of Despond will always be where it is. It is a necessary part of the journey. Similarly, Cummings implies that the Enormous

Room is "necessary," although he hopes that "In the course of the next ten thousand years it may be possible to find the Delectable Mountains without going to prison" (p. 309). We need only recall the ultimate plight of Bunyan's Ignorance, the erstwhile traveling-companion of Christian and Hopeful—who had entered the King's Highway unlawfully from the Country of Conceit, to realize the full significance of the Enormous Room as a purging-place. He and Cummings' "Mr. A.," in their smug complacency and self-confidence, are one-of-a-kind. Neither will enter the gates of the kingdom, although each thinks that he will.

There remains the question of obscenity in *The Enormous Room.* Could Cummings have succeeded, as reviewer D. K. Lamb put it, "without being so gratuitously filthy"? Had William Thackeray lived to read *The Enormous Room,* he would unquestionably have called it "filthy in thought, furious, raging, obscene," as he described *Gulliver's Travels* to a group of nineteenth-century ladies. But happily, such a view of "filthiness" has been demonstrated to be superficial, and despite the persistence of a few critics in reading Swift as personal history, Professors Landa, Ehrenpreis, and others have taught us that to regard *Travels into Several Remote Nations of the World* as evidence of coprophilia in Swift is itself madness. Thus, while it is important to comprehend the meaning of the excrement in Houyhnhnmland, it is trivial to be offended by its odor. Without insisting upon the parallel between the pilgrimages of Bunyan's Christian and Swift's ironic Gulliver,[15] I would nevertheless agree with Professor Monk,[16] who sees a "grim joke" in Gulliver himself being "the supreme instance of a creature smitten with pride."

The significance of such a view for readers of Cummings is this: Gulliver, in his rationalistic pride, is no longer able to smell his fellow human beings without experiencing a wave of nauseating disgust. Having lived in the superrational "civilization" of the horses, he finds the odor of human beings altogether repugnant. Cummings' twentieth-century pilgrim provides us with an alternative. In a world of rationalistic, superscientific, deodorized, Nujolneeding Gullivers, he found it necessary for his salvation to escape into a community of odorous human beings. He discovered them by being imprisoned among them in the Enormous Room.

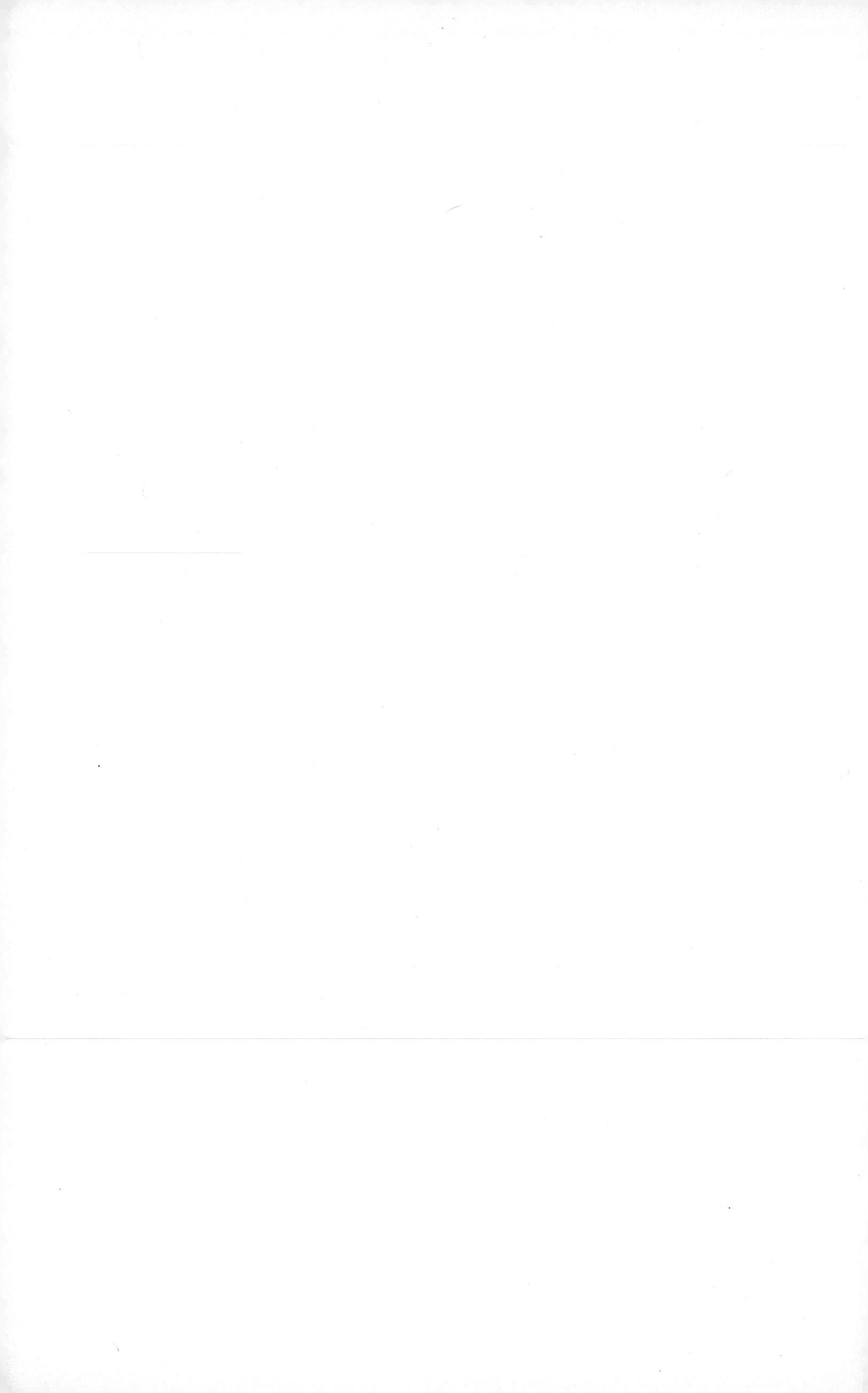

Notes

CHAPTER ONE

1. *John Bunyan: Mechanick Preacher* (New York, 1934).

2. *Millennium and Utopia* (Berkeley, 1948).

3. *The Quest for Paradise: Europe and the American Moral Imagination* (Urbana, 1961).

4. For an interesting recent survey of the wilderness theme, see George Williams, *Wilderness and Paradise in Christian Thought* (New York, 1962).

5. New York: Collier Books, 1961.

6. References by Covey to "Plantonic" Light, the "Ptolematic" universe, "Ann" Bradstreet, Jonathan "Edward," Roger "William," "Pery" Miller, and Bunyan's "Christina" are symptomatic of his somewhat careless approach to a complex subject.

7. *The Kingdom of Basaruah, and Three Unpublished Letters*, ed. with an Introduction by Richard Schlatter (Cambridge, Mass., 1946).

8. For a discussion of intellectual conceptions of gardening in medieval and later England, see Nan Fairbrother, *Men and Gardens* (New York, 1956); and for early colonial conceptions of the wilderness, see Alan Heimert, "Puritanism, the Wilderness, and the Frontier," *New England Quarterly*, XXVI (1953), 361–82.

9. Until the end of the eighteenth century, *The Pilgrim's Progress* was read no more in America than were some of his other works such as *Grace Abounding* and *The Holy War*. It was only in the nineteenth century that interest narrowed to *The Pilgrim's Progress*. For details of publication in this country, see my "Publication of John Bunyan's Works in America," *New York Public Library Bulletin* (December, 1962), which includes a checklist of American editions of Bunyan's works to 1830.

10. The concept of the American wilderness "was not, as it

were, carried to America on the *Mayflower* or the *Arbella,* but came out of that wilderness itself." Heimert, p. 361.

11. Edwin Honig, *Dark Conceit: The Making of Allegory* (Cambridge, Mass., 1960), p. 100.

12. *Theopolis Americana, an Essay on the Golden Street of the Holy City. Publishing a Testimony against the Corruptions of the Market-Place, With Some good Hopes of Better Things to be yet seen in the American World . . .* (Boston, 1710). Mather acknowledges his indebtedness to Sewall in an interesting Dedication. The work was first read at Sewall's house in 1709. Sewall himself had earlier seen the colonies as the obvious and likely site for the New Jerusalem in his interesting *Phaenomena Quaedam Apocalyptica,* a work which obviously inspired Mather. See also Mather's *The City of Refuge* (Boston, 1716), and *India Christiana* (Boston, 1721), not to mention the *Magnalia . . . ,* for elaboration of his views of the millennium. Although Sewall was directly responsible for the first American edition of *The Pilgrim's Progress* (1681), I find no evidence that either of the Mathers had read it. The itinerant bookseller John Dunton had recommended its sale during his visit to the colonies. Covey asserts that Increase Mather "licensed" the first reprint of *The Pilgrim's Progress,* but he offers no evidence for this assertion. The probable reason why many of the prominent colonists did not read Bunyan is the same as for Dryden and his contemporaries: such works were beneath the notice of gentlemen.

13. Honig, p. 163.

14. *A Commentary on the General Prologue to the Canterbury Tales* (New York, 1954), esp. Chap. II, "The Pilgrimages."

15. I am indebted to a lecture by R. W. B. Lewis for the image of the clown. What I say about the clown-as-pilgrim, is, of course, not what Mr. Lewis might say.

16. For some few souls, the irrepressible conflict took on the nature of a Holy War, but the events of Reconstruction must have persuaded even the most recalcitrant that Satan had not yet been bound. If the War was cataclysmic, it did not introduce the awaited millennium. See Timothy L. Smith, *Revivalism and Social Reform* (New York, 1957).

17. *The Education of Henry Adams* (Boston, 1918), p. 88.

18. Ibid., pp. 75, 433.

19. Quoted in Reinhold Niebuhr, *The Nature and Destiny of Man* (New York, 1948), I, 126.

20. "He had that sense, or inward prophecy,—which a young man had better never have been born than not to have, and a mature man had better die at once than utterly to relinquish,—that we are not doomed to creep on forever in the old bad way, but that, this very now, there are the harbingers abroad of a golden era." *The Complete Novels and Selected Tales of Nathaniel Hawthorne,* ed. Norman Holmes Pearson (New York, 1937), p. 350.

CHAPTER TWO

1. *Dark Conceit,* p. 3.

2. Quoted in an undated advertisement printed in the 1849 edition.

3. William B. Kinney, editor of the Newark *Sentinel,* also quoted in the 1849 edition.

4. E. H. Gillett, *History of the Presbyterian Church in the United States of America* (2 vols.; Philadelphia, 1864), I, 453.

5. Ibid., p. 457.

6. "New England: Published for the Author, 1843." The work was entered at the district court of Rhode Island by Williams Thayer, who may have been merely the publisher, and about whom I have failed to uncover any information. Conceivably the author was a woman. (See note 12, below.)

7. Whoever the author was, he had read Hawthorne's "Celestial Railroad." In an interesting note on the last page, he states: "The 'Celestial Railroad' was not in print at the time this was written. The mention of the Bridge at the Slough of Despond, is an accidental coincidence."

8. Another prototype is the first edition of Weeks' *Pilgrim's Progress in the Nineteenth Century,* which appeared in 1824–26. However, it was only in his final 1849 edition that Weeks broadened the scope of his attack, although in doing so he weakened the effectiveness of the original. Some of the objects of attack in *Pilgrim's Progress in the Last Days* include: liberalism, rationalism, orthodoxy *per se,* political expediency, tyranny, revivalism, transcendentalism, slavery, race prejudice, segregation, libertinism, and progress.

9. Racial prejudice, for example, as well as the problems of segregation, is treated, as on pp. 80–84.

10. Hawthorne's "Celestial Railroad" is the only other work of this nature which deals successfully with at least two of these conventional objects of attack, although almost all the other "American Pilgrim's Progresses" try to do so.

11. To put it conversely: one would search in vain for any nineteenth-century American adaptations which did not attack liberalism in church and state. Furthermore, there are no comic *Pilgrim's Progresses* in this period. The work was sacrosanct, apparently, until after the Civil War. I have found no American parodies (there are numerous English parodies), and the only "light" use of *The Pilgrim's Progress* in this country before the Civil War is the Delano-Nahl pamphlet *The Miner's Progress* (Sacramento, 1853). It would appear that the Far West, beginning with Delano and continuing with Clemens, could claim sole rights to the first ridiculing of Bunyan in America.

12. In one skirmish certain treacherous servants are described firing out of the windows of the House Beautiful itself at the Abolitionist army (p. 69). The description of the two armies mustering for the fray is interesting. The standard for Pro-Slavery's army was an eagle bearing off a sheep, with the motto "Might Makes Right" (p. 62). At the front of Christian Abolition's army was "a band of intrepid women led on by Charity to the very front" (p. 61). Conceivably the book was written by a woman who wished to retain her anonymity. One of the most powerful pieces of artillery in the Abolition camp, incidentally, was a "piece of ordinance called the Liberator, whose deep thunders opened the battle . . ." (p. 67).

13. Segregation is dramatized in the speech of Discontent, who claims that where he wishes to go all is order and subordination. "If there are any colored persons there, they go by themselves. Only give them the time of day [he says to Prejudice], and speak civilly, to keep them contented—but association! Oh no!" (p. 83).

14. His arch-antagonist is still Pro-Slavery.

15. *The California Pilgrim: A Series of Lectures* (Sacramento: Solomon Alter, 1853).

16. *California as She was: As She is: As She is to be. A discourse Delivered at the First Church of Christ, in Sixth Street, Sacramento City; on the Occasion of the Annual Thanksgiving, November 30, 1850* (Sacramento City, 1850).

17. An illuminating discussion of the significance of Whitman's

view of the West as a promised garden may be found in Henry Nash Smith's *Virgin Land* (New York: Vintage Books, 1957), Bk. I, Chap. IV.

18. See Robert M. York, *George B. Cheever, Religious and Social Reformer, 1807–1890,* University of Maine Studies, Second Series, No. 69 (Orono, Maine, 1955), for a survey of Cheever's life and his principal activities. York is less interested in Cheever's lifelong devotion to Bunyan than in some of his other intellectual influences, and fails to record three of Cheever's published works of a Bunyanesque nature: *A Reel in a Bottle, The Hill Difficulty,* and *Waymarks of a Pilgrimage.*

19. York cites letters of Cheever and others indicating the enormous turn-away crowds which attended these lectures when he first gave them in New York. The published version of the *Lectures* went into a third edition by 1845, a sixth by 1846, a seventh by 1847, an eighth by 1849, and subsequent editions throughout the rest of the century, not to mention innumerable English editions. York was unaware of this publishing record, apparently.

20. Cheever compares the early American settlers with Christian in this edited version of "Mourt's relation": *Journal of the Pilgrims at Plymouth in New England . . .* (New York, 1849); and he cites Bunyan frequently in the latter pages of one of his Abolitionist diatribes, *God Against Slavery . . .* (New York, 1857), although Bunyan himself had no informed opinions about the matter of slavery.

21. Subtitled *The Adventures of Two of the King's Seamen in a Voyage to the Celestial Country* (New York, 1852). The curious title apparently did not prevent the book from becoming a popular seller. In a later, somewhat revised version, Cheever simplified the title to *The Log-Book of a Voyage to the Celestial Country* (New York: A. O. Armstrong & Son, 1885). In the preface to the 1885 edition, the author notes that the original work was "prepared" around 1850 (I have been unable to trace any edition before 1852) and that "several editions were published by the firm of Charles Scribner" under the title *A Reel in a Bottle. . . .* This title was "afterwards deemed too technical and exclusive." There was at least one English edition, and apparently at least four American editions of the work, although Cheever's biographer, Robert M. York, does not mention the work at all.

22. See York, pp. 70, 114.

23. It is not unlikely that Cheever had read his classmate Hawthorne's "The Celestial Railroad." Cheever had himself conducted a running battle with the railroads, arising from their persistence in operating on the Sabbath (see York, pp. 133–34). On Cheever's *allegorical* railroad, "any traveller might spend a year or more at any intermediate station, as at the great town of Vanity Fair . . ." (p. 52).

24. For Cheever's impassioned activities as an abolitionist, and for the details of his connection with Henry Ward Beecher, Harriet Beecher Stowe, and her husband Calvin Stowe (also a Bowdoin classmate), see York.

25. It would be tedious to recount at length the many adventures and moral lessons which fill the pages of Cheever's voluminous work. Those which have been noted here are characteristic of the whole. One further encounter is interesting because it may have been intended as a parody of *Moby Dick*. The Pilgrims meet a whaler whose captain is prepossessed with catching whales: "If you could look into my heart," he says, "I believe you would see nothing but a whale there. What can a man do? It is my destiny to have a whale" (p. 302). Cheever's lifelong interest in American literature would make it seem likely that he had read *Moby Dick* critically, and the fact that Melville's work appeared in 1851, when Cheever was presumably writing his own novel, would lend credence to this hypothesis.

26. Cheever's *Lectures on "The Pilgrim's Progress" and on the Life and Times of John Bunyan* was neither the first nor the most extensive American commentary on Bunyan, but it was probably the most popular.

27. Although York did not mention it, Cheever's father, Nathaniel, published Maine's only known edition of *The Pilgrim's Progress* (Hallowell, 1817). Furthermore, Cheever's mother was instrumental in guiding her son down the narrow paths of conservatism, and there is evidence that for her *The Pilgrim's Progress* was a principal guidebook. Interestingly, when young George's faith was on the point of wavering at Bowdoin, he sent desperately for a copy of *The Pilgrim's Progress* to bolster his faith and to aid in his conversion. York, p. 31.

28. The curious circumstance that three members of a single class at Bowdoin College should become three of the principal

"champions" of Bunyan's works in their generation may be more than a coincidence. Calvin Stowe alleged that no book meant more to him; Hawthorne's uses of Bunyan are discussed here and in Chapter III. Cheever is the third classmate. The only direct Bowdoin influence which I have investigated is the unquestionably pervasive influence of the ideas of Professor T. C. Upham, instructor in Moral Theology; but a cursory examination of Upham's works reveals not a single reference to Bunyan or his works. Thus one would conclude that it was simply and inevitably this generation's lot to be "exposed" to Bunyan during childhood. The exposure rarely wore off.

29. *Modern Pilgrims: Showing the Improvements in Travel, and the Newest Methods of Reaching the Celestial City*, 2 vols. (Boston, 1855).

30. "The plan of my book was suggested to me by Hawthorne's inimitable allegory, 'The Celestial Railroad . . .' " (prefatory letter to Rev. Francis Wayland, President of Brown University).

31. See John Newton Brown, *History of the American Baptist Publication Society from its Origin in 1824, to its Thirty-second Anniversary in 1856* (Philadelphia, [18—]), p. 13. John Newton Brown was an indefatigable distributor of Bunyan's works in America, editing four or five sets for the society during the 1850's. He was known for the "Calvinistic" nature of his professed faith. Brown was also editor of an early religious encyclopedia—*Fessenden & Co.'s Encyclopedia of Religious Knowledge* . . . (Brattleboro, Vermont, 1837), which is especially useful for its many entries concerning current theories of the millennium.

32. One is reminded of Mark Twain's astute observation of a similarly pompous bishop who was considering booking passage on the *Quaker City:* "He looked as though he were waiting for a vacancy in the Trinity."

33. Why Wood, a Baptist, should indicate as much is difficult to explain, unless it is because both churches are essentially Calvinistic.

34. I have by no means exhausted this genre by describing a few examples of it. In addition to the works noticed here (including Cheever's many variations on the theme), I might mention *The Adventures of Search for Life, A Bunyanic Narrative, as Detailed by Himself*, a Universalist tract issued at Portland, Maine, in 1838, and written by D. J. Mendell; *The City of Sin, and Its Capture by*

Immanuel's Army (New York, 1857), an allegory based on Bunyan's *Holy War*, apocalyptic in nature, and introduced by Cheever; and William M. Bryant's *A Narrative of the Voyage of Life, in the Brig Convert, from the Village of Newness-of-Life, to the Port of Endless Joy, in the Empire of Glory* (Biddeford, Maine, 1859).

CHAPTER THREE

1. *The Complete Works of Nathaniel Hawthorne,* Fireside Edition (Boston and New York, 1909), VII, 537. The passage is in the form of a brief memorandum in the English Notebooks of 1854.

2. When Hawthorne encountered underbrush during his walks in the woods he was driven into a state of despair. *The American Notebooks by Nathaniel Hawthorne,* ed. Randall Stewart (New Haven, 1932), p. 159.

3. I have found no evidence to suggest that Hawthorne had read widely in Bunyan. His allusions are repeatedly to either the First Part or the Second Part of *The Pilgrim's Progress.*

4. Norman Holmes Pearson, ed., *The Complete Novels and Selected Tales of Nathaniel Hawthorne* (New York, 1937), viii. Subsequent page references in this chapter are to this edition unless otherwise noted.

5. George Offor, ed., *The Works of John Bunyan* (3 vols.; Glasgow, 1855), III, 104.

6. In *The Blithedale Romance,* Coverdale's retreat is halfway up a pine tree, which "being ancient, rose high above the rest of the wood." The pine tree itself is situated "off the track" through the woods, and Coverdale's actual position in the tree is exactly between the root and the topmost bough. In this position he views the world with the "eyes of the Devil." The tree offers him a secluded position which resembles a "kind of leafy cave, high upward into the air." If pine trees represent, as they seem to do, the rigid and unbending view of life of the first-generation Puritans, then the difference between Coverdale's midway position in his Blithedale pine tree, and Fanshawe's position at the top of the trees which "seemed to soar to heaven," is significant. Fanshawe is Ellen's deliverer in an almost godlike sense. Coverdale's chosen position as a kind of halfway participant in the transcendental utopian experiment, along with his return to the Boston conservatives for advice, finds perfect expression in his mid-position in the tree.

7. The most complete recent study of the problems encountered by Hawthorne in his attempt to merge the "actual" with the imaginative may be found in Donald A. Campbell, "A Critical Analysis of Nathaniel Hawthorne's *The Blithedale Romance*" (doctoral dissertation, Yale University, 1960). Randall Stewart has also noted Hawthorne's "increasing disposition to deal critically with the social problems of [his] own time." *Nathaniel Hawthorne* (New Haven, 1948), p. 71.

8. Letters frequently repeat the analogy. See Julian Hawthorne, *Hawthorne and his Wife* (2 vols.; Cambridge, Mass., 1884), I. The prefatory sketch, "The Old Manse," continues the imagery, likening the garden to that of Eden, and his study to Eve's bower. See *Mosses,* pp. 22, 26. The first word taught to Una, the child born in the Old Manse, was "Adam." See also *Notebooks,* Aug. 5, 1842.

For a more general, and highly perceptive discussion of Adamic imagery in Hawthorne and elsewhere, see R. W. B. Lewis, *The American Adam* (Chicago, 1955). Mr. Lewis' observation that the characteristic situation in Hawthorne's fiction is that of the "Emersonian figure, the man of hope, who by some frightful mischance has stumbled into the time-burdened world of Jonathan Edwards" (p. 113), is especially relevant to my discussion.

9. One of the most perceptive analyses of this central problem is in Edwin Honig, *Dark Conceit,* a work I have had occasion to refer to earlier. Honig describes Hawthorne's need to create his own "authority" as an allegorist reformulating the methods inherited from Bunyan and Spenser. See Chap. IV, pp. 91–112.

10. Campbell, pp. 103–4.

11. O. B. Frothingham, *George Ripley* (Boston, 1884), p. 111: "The disciples were gathered, the iniquity of the world was full; the angel had put the trumpet to his lips." Blithedale is frequently referred to as a millennial paradise. See, for example, Pearson, *The Complete Novels,* pp. 452, 475.

12. Chillingworth's New England mission is also figuratively described in walking imagery, for he "tread[s] behind [Dimmesdale's] every footstep" (p. 185). His own intentions are described in the following phrase, characteristic of the novel: "The intellect of Roger Chillingworth had now a sufficiently plain path before it" (p. 171). A metaphor of walking is also used to describe in detail Chillingworth's relationship to Dimmesdale: "Thus Roger Chillingworth scrutinized his patient carefully, both as he saw him in his

ordinary life, keeping an accustomed pathway in the range of thoughts familiar to him, and as he appeared when thrown amidst other moral scenery, the novelty of which might call out something new to the surface of his character" (p. 157). Furthermore, it is when he is taking his walks that he encounters Hester and Pearl "in a remote part of the peninsula," and he continues to take Dimmesdale on "long walks on the sea-shore, or in the forest," during which he subjects the frail minister to his penetrating spiritual examinations.

13. Hawthorne's use of the bypath is frequent, and entirely consistent, from his first to his last works. The major denouement of *Fanshawe* occurs on a bypath in a forest; the carefully described bypath down which Hester lures Dimmesdale will be discussed in this chapter; Coverdale has a private bypath of his own; Zenobia strays from the path—the list could be multiplied indefinitely. In Hawthorne's imagination, the bypath was almost always in a pine woods, and it consistently symbolized moral chaos. Hawthorne may have been familiar with Bunyan's *The Heavenly Footman,* and passages such as this: "Beware of by-paths; take heed thou dost not turn into those lanes which lead out of the way. There are crooked paths, paths in which men go astray, paths that lead to death and damnation, but take heed of all those." Henri Talon, ed., *God's Knotty Log: Selected Writings of John Bunyan* (New York, 1961), pp. 34–35.

14. Offor ed., III, 166.

15. Arthur Dimmesdale's characteristic gesture!

16. No passage in Bunyan fascinated Hawthorne more than this one, for it reappears throughout his work. In "My Kinsman, Major Molineaux," a ferryman delivers the young traveler into the City; in "The Celestial Railroad," the climactic scene involves a journey down the river with a satanic ferryman; in *The Blithedale Romance*, the same passage is referred to in connection with Hollingsworth's ultimate fate. Hawthorne returned to the image again when he described Ethan Brand's limekiln.

17. See Hawthorne's portrayal of Eliot in *Grandfather's Chair.* " 'Treat these sons of the forest as men and brethren,' [Eliot] would say; 'and let us endeavor to make them Christians. Their forefathers were of that chosen race whom God delivered from Egyptian bondage. . . . Here was a Bible for the Indians. Those long-lost descendants of the ten tribes of Israel would now learn the history of their forefathers.' " *Complete Works*, IV, 474–75.

18. The obvious identification of Clifford and Hepzibah in *The House of the Seven Gables,* with Christian and Hopeful fleeing Doubting Castle (Judge Pyncheon having become Giant Despair [p. 394]), is yet another example of Hawthorne's habit of turning directly to Bunyan as a major source of imagery at crucial points in the development of his stories. The moment has arrived for Clifford to escape into the world. Judge Pyncheon, Clifford's literal and symbolic jailer, has collapsed from the characteristic Pyncheon paroxysm, and the House (always prison-like) may now safely be abandoned, or so Clifford has persuaded himself in his deluded mental state. In the First Part of *The Pilgrim's Progress,* Christian had recalled at the eleventh hour that he had in his bosom a key called Promise, which would open any lock in Doubting Castle. He uses it to escape with Hopeful. In Part Two of *The Pilgrim's Progress,* Great-heart cuts off the head of Giant Despair, and Doubting Castle is demolished. Not so with the House of the Seven Gables. We should recall, finally, that just as Doubting Castle was on a byway off the King's Highway, so was the House of the Seven Gables on Pyncheon Street, which had become a byway.

19. Offor ed., III, 92.

20. See note 5, above, for significances of this image.

21. In *The Blithedale Romance,* Hawthorne once again alludes to Eliot's visionary theories, when he has the principal Utopians meet frequently near a large slab of rock in the forest which was "Eliot's pulpit"; it was here that, within the bubble of their illusion, the principals conversed and argued. What Hawthorne suggested was an ironic repetition of history.

22. See, for example, William Van O'Connor, "Conscious Naïveté in *The Blithedale Romance,*" *Revue des Langues vivantes,* XX (1943), 37–45; Frank Davidson, "Towards a Re-evaluation of *The Blithedale Romance,*" *New England Quarterly,* XXV (1952), 374–82; and especially Frederick C. Crews, "A New Reading of *The Blithedale Romance,*" *American Literature,* XXIX (1957), 147–70.

23. I am aware that searching for literary borrowings is beset with difficulties, but I hope to demonstrate that, in this instance, *The Pilgrim's Progress* should be no more ignored as a likely source for characterization in *Blithedale* than, say, Madame de Staël's *Corinne.* See H. Arlin Turner, "Hawthorne's Literary Borrowings," *Publications of the Modern Language Association of America,* LI (Nov. 1936), 426–29.

24. Offor ed., III, 176.

15. "It was never a book for juvenile readers alone. On its first appearance it was read . . . by men and women as well as by girls and boys." Katharine Anthony, *Louisa May Alcott* (New York, 1938), p. 172.

16. The objection could be made to this analysis that Miss Alcott probably had the Second Part of *The Pilgrim's Progress* in mind, where the pilgrims are actually female, although led by Great-heart. Actually, however, Miss Alcott does not rely upon the images of the Second Part of *The Pilgrim's Progress* with the single exception of Mrs. March's emergency trip to Washington. Her companion, Mr. Brooke, is likened at that time to Great-heart. But Mrs. March, unlike Christiana, leaves her family at home, and the focus is entirely upon the "pilgrims" left there, not on the mother's journey. All other references to Bunyan in *Little Women* are to the First Part of *Pilgrim's Progress.*

17. Whereas the relationship between Mrs. March and her children is depicted by the metaphor of a sun towards which little flowers turn (p. 171), the relationship between the invalid father and his daughters is depicted as follows: "Like bees swarming after their queen, mother and daughters hovered about Mr. March the next day, neglecting everything to look at, wait upon, and listen to the new invalid, who was in a fair way to be killed by kindness" (p. 326). Perhaps the crushing unimportance of Father March was pointed out to Miss Alcott before she wrote the second part of *Little Women,* for that book begins with an apology for him. Nevertheless, the "quiet scholar, sitting among his books" barely manages to get into the Second Part of *Little Women,* and his ineffectual character does not change.

18. *Little Women,* p. 205.

19. Jo is compared specifically with Christian (in the Second Part, p. 282), and she is like him also in the quality of her masculinity. She is the head of the family, she understands the nature of the pilgrimage, and ultimately, through her writing, she defines the quality of the family's experiences, specifically in the context of the house in which they live. Bronson Alcott's remark about Louisa, when she left Concord to become a war nurse in Washington, is appropriate at this point. He allegedly said, "My only son has gone to war."

20. Jo's final act before she marries Professor Bhaer at the conclusion of the Second Part of *Little Women* is to show him a

poem she has written which defines and summarizes the life and character of each pilgrim, using the image of "Four little [doll] chests" in the garret of the March house. Having consecrated the life of each girl, and having buried each, in a manner of speaking, in a chest in the garret, Jo tears up the poem and accepts her new life with Bhaer.

21. "Hillside," the house on Lexington Road, Concord, where Louisa lived from her thirteenth to her sixteenth year, and which was "immortalized as the background of *Little Women*" (Anthony, *Louisa May Alcott,* p. 57), was the object of pilgrimages even in Louisa's own lifetime, ultimately becoming a shrine, which it remains to this day.

22. Contemporary biographers of Louisa May Alcott, like Katharine Anthony, find it necessary to protest, "It has been my observation that all books written about the subject of this biography, whatever their nature and purpose, are classed as children's books. The following life of Louisa May Alcott, it may therefore be stated here, was not written for children." Anthony, p. vii.

23. Sylvia Yule, the heroine of Miss Alcott's first novel, *Moods* (1864), considered herself a homeless creature. Father Yule, in that work, resembles Father March in *Little Women* in that both are ineffectual, retiring failures.

24. The real poor—the Boston Irish—remain on the periphery of the novel as objects of charity, curiosity, or disgust. The German immigrants come off a little better, but even they are described as suitable recipients of leftover meals because, as Amy puts it, "Germans like messes."

25. *Bronson Alcott's Fruitlands,* compiled by Clara Endicott Sears, with *Transcendental Wild Oats,* by Louisa May Alcott (Boston and New York, 1915).

26. *Ibid.,* p. 150.

CHAPTER FIVE

1. Page references are to the Jonathan Cape edition. London, 1928.

2. May 28, 1922.

3. June 4, 1922.

4. May 17, 1922.

5. *On Native Grounds* (New York, 1942), p. 345.

6. Reviewers at the time generally failed to take note of Cummings' scheme, although it is obvious enough with such chapter titles as "I Begin a Pilgrimage," "A Pilgrim's Progress," and "Apollyon." A recent critic of the novel, Kingsley Widmer, feels that "while the use of Bunyan and the pilgrimage is only partial, and probably could not justify the ingenuity of systematic exposition, it does give elements of order at several levels to the poetic narrative." "Timeless Prose," *Twentieth Century Literature,* IV (1958), 6. What I wish to suggest is that the spiritual pilgrimage actually begins in La Ferté Macé; that "timelessness" is of its essence; and that such a notion is not contradictory to Bunyan's allegory understood on its grander spiritual level.

7. For the most comprehensive recent summary of the significance of the Infernal Trinity—"the captains of the hosts of hell which war against the soul"—see Samuel C. Chew, *The Pilgrimage of Life* (New Haven and London, 1962), pp. 70–78. The "instruments of [Apollyon's] power" in *The Enormous Room* were "Fear, Women, and Sunday" (p. 162).

8. Kenneth Burke, *A Grammar of Motives* (New York, 1945), pp. 300–303.

9. In his study of "Change in the Poetry of E. E. Cummings," *PMLA,* LXX (1955), 913–33, Rudolphe Von Abele noticed that "Cummings sensed the satiric potentialities of the interdicted imagery of sex and excrement" (p. 928), and that as a consequence critics have "perhaps inevitabl[y]" called him "infantile" and "adolescent" for it. Von Abele limits his discussion, of course, to Cummings' poetry.

10. The Count's name carries out the book's general pattern of allegorical names. "Bragard" sounds like "braggart"; his initials, "F.A.," suggest *fanfaron.*

11. I disagree with Kazin's interpretation (*On Native Grounds,* p. 325): "The enormous room, by its very remoteness from war, mirrored and intensified its inherent meaninglessness; it became a maze in which men clawed each other to escape or to keep their reason. And the central theme of their imprisonment was chaos." I do not deny that the "profoundly irrational" pervades the atmosphere of the enormous room, but I assert that a religious meaning must be assigned to it. Cummings' "vision of the universe" is not "surrealist," as Kazin claims. It is incongruously Christian.

12. Cummings' prepossession with olfactory images serves in

part to explain his deliberate and early use of the sonnet form to describe prostitutes. The sonnet sequences of *Tulips and Chimneys* bear more than a superficial resemblance to "Holy Sonnets." They are deliberately religious in tone while they deal with subjects which are physically offensive.

13. Count Bragard's hypocrisy is intensified when we recall that Cummings admired Cézanne and expressionism, his own role in *The Enormous Room* being that of a semiabstract painter. Bragard, the false painter, draws horses for money; Cummings, the true painter, portrays a gallery of divine subjects. His "portraits" are drawn with the same nervous calligraphy evident in the line drawings he was publishing at this time.

14. The pun here conveys Cummings' central ironic intention.

15. Calhoun Winton, in "Conversion on the Road to Houyhnhnmland," *The Sewanee Review,* LXVIII (Winter 1960), 20–33, maintains that *Gulliver's Travels* "intentionally echoes . . . *A* [sic] *Pilgrim's Progress.*" Gulliver, in his view, is "a sort of eighteenth-century English Everyman whose pilgrimage from a position of complete religious ignorance culminates with 'conversion' . . . to . . . the reasonable faith of the hyper-reasonable horses, in Houyhnhnmland's new Eden." Swift is not to be mistaken for Gulliver, whose conversion is to be understood ironically.

16. Samuel Holt Monk, "The Pride of Lemuel Gulliver," *The Sewanee Review,* LXIII (Winter 1955), 48–71.

INDEX

Indiana University Humanities Series No. 61

INDIANA UNIVERSITY PRESS

$3.00 | 22s.